Driving Ambition

Alan Jones
and Keith Botsford

Driving Ambition

Stanley Paul

London Melbourne Sydney Auckland Johannesburg

Stanley Paul & Co. Ltd

An imprint of the Hutchinson Publishing Group

17–21 Conway Street, London W1

Hutchinson Group (Australia) Pty Ltd
30–32 Cremorne Street, Richmond South, Victoria 3121
PO Box 151, Broadway, New South Wales 2007

Hutchinson Group (NZ) Ltd
32–34 View Road, PO Box 40–086, Glenfield, Auckland 10

Hutchinson Group (SA) (Pty) Ltd
PO Box 337, Bergvlei 2012, South Africa

First published 1981
Reprinted 1981 (three times)
© Alan Jones and Keith Botsford 1981

Set in Linotron Century Roman

Printed in Great Britain
by the Anchor Press Ltd
and bound by Wm Brendon and Son,
both of Tiptree, Essex

ISBN 0 09 146240 1

The majority of the photographs are reproduced by
courtesy of Nigel Snowdon and Diana Burnett. Others
were supplied by Alan Jones, Peter Tempest and Shadow
Cars.

To Beverley
for helping make it possible
and putting up with me, and
to the memory of my father, where
it all started

Contents

By Way of Foreword

Part 1: The Making of a 'Different Sort of Being'   7

Part 2: Formula One, But Not All is Roses   46

Part 3: A.J. Settles into the Formula One Family   72

Part 4: The Profession, Seen from the Top   107

Part 5: The Whole Complexity of Life   123

Championship Diary 1980   151

Afterword   166

Career   167

By Way of Foreword

All oral autobiographies are a two-way street. The writer elicits, questions, probes, insists; the subject talks, meanders, evades, relaxes, concentrates. The final result is an organized conversation, reworked and transformed from its inchoate state into an order, a style and a language all its own. This book is the product of some thirty hours of taped talk, transcribed, edited and crafted. What A.J. says in it is his, what I say is mine. He gave unstintingly, but not on all subjects equally willingly.

That is because the sport, though public, is one full of reticences and unformulated and unspoken taboos. From the start, I aimed to create a totally different kind of book on the sport and the people who form its inner family. I wanted to avoid – which came easily to me, as I am not a natural enthusiast – the kind of gung-ho, insider literature which prevails in motor racing. If A.J. and I have succeeded at all, it is because he had the will and the intelligence and I had many questions unanswered in my own mind.

Both A.J. and his immediate 'family', the Williams team, were extremely helpful, but the main burden obviously fell on A.J. himself. As he acknowledges, he thinks more than he says, and has 'neither the time nor the desire to put myself into words': that this book is as revealing as it is, not only of Alan Jones, but of the sport, speaks much for his integrity and intelligence.

K.B.

Part 1

The Making of a 'Different Sort of Being'

Most people are bloody ignorant about my sport. I can live with that. They think drivers are people in a bit of a hurry; they jump into a racing car, go off round the track doing their ten-tenths or better and then afterwards they kiss all the birds hello and goodbye and go home, and that's that. Like pigs can fly.

A.J.'s sport is Formula One racing. This book is an attempt to tell those who don't know what the sport is about what it is like from the inside.

Consider some of the complexities to which A.J. will return later:

The sort of person I am on the track is totally different from my other personality. On the farm, any resemblance between myself and a racing driver is pure coincidence, but when I have to race that day, I am, literally, a different being.

Or:

If it were just a matter of getting into the car and going quick, there'd be a lot more drivers up and around where I am. The really good ones win races in the slowest times, not the quickest.

Or:

There are pressures that derive from the extreme competitiveness of the sport. I am constitutionally incapable of getting into a car and being jovial and relaxed. I cannot take it easy or say it doesn't matter that there are a dozen things wrong with the

7

car. Perhaps my ego won't allow me to do that. I have to be the quickest, I have to be the best. If I'm not, I blow my cool.

Or:

The start of a race is in itself neither joyful nor frightening. It is a commitment. I am there because I choose to be there. I do not sit in my car wondering what I'm doing there or wishing to get out. I do whatever is necessary to get the best result. I'm aware that I'm playing it all down. Of course you are surrounded, of course you may be scared at the start; but, being in that manic, committed stage, I am so hyped up, the competitive edge is so sharp, that I know I am going to have a go, regardless of the risk.

Or:

I've had races entirely without jubilation or excitement, even though I've won. That's the difference with a race seen from the inside and the outside.

Or:

If you could imagine sitting in the cockpit of a Formula One car, like almost anyone else whose experience has been limited to a road car, you would be both exhilarated and scared out of your wits. Probably more the latter. What I do, and the speed at which I do it, seems to me absolutely routine.

Or:

I don't feel flattered when I'm complimented for some abstract quality like bravery, in that I go fast and I'm not frightened.

Or:

Drivers don't question why they're racing. The top ones find it comes so normally they believe anyone could do what they do. When it comes that easily, they feel guilty about it.

Or:

Desire and envy play a part in moving any driver. If someone is on pole and I'm not, I feel both envy and desire: I envy him his position and I want to deprive him of the advantage he has gained.

Or:

Rain is something else. The danger lies not in your skidding, but in your ability to anticipate: if something happens ahead of you and there is a car on the track, you will literally plough into him before you can see him.

Or:

The mind takes over from the body and makes you forget its state of unease. Most of us take our racing very personally and that buries all the problems we face somewhere deep in the subconscious.

Or:

I think it fair to say we're a callous lot about death. If I were killed tomorrow, Frank would probably say, 'That's too bad; A.J. was a bit of a character.' The truth may not be attractive, but it remains true. Frank is in the business of motor racing and in his plans, I am a cog. We are bloody mercenaries and we can't get hysterical every time someone gets killed.

Or:

Today all is commerce and cold blood. Do I approve or disapprove? I don't do either. I recognize things the way they are.

Or:

Drivers are very conscious beings, but the subconscious still plays its part. To go through a corner really fast, a driver has to prepare his subconscious. Yet the preparation of that subconscious is a conscious act. That doesn't mean the fear is not always within us.

Or:

The thought of quitting grows on a driver little by little. He finds himself thinking about it more and more. It seems ever more desirable. He sleeps a little less after each race. He enjoys driving a little less. His edge goes off, his appetite diminishes. Courage comes when a driver recognizes that moment and quits.

Or:

A lot of people say, now I'm World Champion I won't try so hard. But I am not racing to be World Champion, which I am and which can't be gainsaid. I go racing because I still want to, and because I want people to respect me for that.

Or:

A lot of my life has been repression. I check myself a lot. In feeling, certainly. I was a kid who went dancing and wouldn't ask the girl to dance in case she rejected me. Pride is involved, and insecurity. Stubbornness, an inability to take things as they come, or to let my true feelings show.

Or:

I have to sit on myself because I know what I want and where I'm going in life. My biggest want is to be on top, and that means sitting on the beast in me to get there.

Or, finally:

So far, I have expressed my life in my racing, and who I am will not come out until I've finished.

Those words, which finish the book, and those which have pre-

ceded it, indicate the world of Formula One is complex, self-critical, conscious, intelligent and unique. The rest is an anatomy of the sport and those who practise it.

It has its own natural order, its own progression. But first, a definition. Formula One is the top of the sport, and a 'formula' is just a set of rules governing the nature, the power and the dimensions of A.J.'s car.

It is generally some years before a driver, any driver, however considerable his talent, reaches Formula One. It took A.J. some five years; and then some three before he made his mark.

Getting your bum into a car and driving a car are two very different things. Before you can drive a car, you have to have one. To have one requires ducking and diving; it takes wheeling, dealing and conniving. And that part of motor racing is the bigger part. It's like the bottom six-sevenths of an iceberg – nobody who hasn't hit one knows what it's like. I came to England in 1969 with exactly fifty quid in my pocket and this certainty that what I wanted to do was race motor cars. And another certainty, that I would one day be World Champion.

It wasn't just that my old man didn't have money, though he didn't. It was my conviction that I'd rather make it on my own. Just as well: the old man had all his eggs in one basket, the basket being motor cars. He wasn't the first or the last of the big spenders, just a man who turned spending into an art. There was a time in my childhood when he was both rich and a big-time racing driver in Australia; but whatever he made at one end selling cars, he lost at the other, racing them.

Those were not the days of really professional motor racing. Money hadn't come into the sport: not the way it has today. In the old man's day, if you won a race you got a brand new pair of socks, a dayglo orange see-through shirt or maybe a little tin trophy: none of which pay for sending people around the world to buy brand new Maseratis or to keep two mechanics working full time.

A brief note on Stan Jones, driver from another era. He reappears often in A.J.'s words: as someone to be loved, as an example to be avoided. In 1954, he became the first Aussie to win a grand prix outside his own country – it was in New Zealand – and he was offered a works drive for Ferrari or BRM. In 1958 he won the Australian Grand Prix. A pretty sharp driver, by all accounts; a big, florid man.

Motor racing was in the blood. The old man was good enough to be offered drives for Ferrari and BRM, but he had a young son and a young business. It was Jack Brabham who went to Europe, and what Jack Brabham did, winning three world championships, is history. The truth is, the old man could drive Brabham into the weeds. When Brabham was New South Wales champion and my Dad was Champion of Victoria, they had a grudge race at Fisherman's Bend, just the two of them. When Brabham crossed the finish line, my old man was already out of his car sitting there drinking a Coke. I admire everything Brabham did, but I reckon my old man to have been as good or better.

Racing often runs in families like that: either a father who drove and raced, or a father who had an intimate connexion with cars. Jack Brabham, too, was a Formula One world champion; and an Australian.

I didn't want what happened to my father to happen to me. I didn't want to live under a question mark. My old man died wondering whether he should have gone to Europe or not. For an Australian can win anything at home, but until he meets the best in the world in some formula that's universally recognized, there's still a question mark over him. No question mark over me. I decided I'd go over, give it a good go and if I turned out a failure, I could still look myself in the shaving mirror and say I'd given it a go, had some fun and had some stories to live on. But the old man died with the question mark hanging there.

Now there are people my age in Australia saying, I should have gone over when A.J. went over. That's life. The old man might have been a failure, he might have been a bit of a hero; but if you eliminate question marks from your life, you die happier.

A.J.'s father died in London before his son had made it to the top. It was a painful parting; the son loved the father and raced with and for him. And when he lay in his coffin to be sent back to Australia, A.J. packed a laurel won at Silverstone in with him. Stan Jones' failure – if going broke is a failure – weighed heavily on his son, Alan Stanley Jones, born 2 November 1946.

Selling cars back in those days was like stocking shirts in a haberdashers: you had to have what the customer wanted on your lot. When the Major with his RAF whiskers drives up and says he wants pink upholstery with green stripes, he wants that car right away, in time for a drink at sundown. If you don't have it, he moves along a couple of blocks and buys it from someone else. So the old man had literally hundreds of cars on the lot; his money came from turnover. Which is fine when things are going well. Then came the great credit squeeze: the cars were on the lot but my Dad couldn't pay for them. He went under, like thousands of others. He had to start up again, just to keep his head above water and pay off the receivers. I found his fate instructive: the smart man doesn't put all his eggs in one basket.

We all take lessons from our parents, even if it only hits your subconscious; and part of the art of learning is to be able to look facts in the face, analysing them and either accepting or rejecting them. You get used to taking short cuts; and the biggest short cuts are the things you learn from life and your parents. I didn't grow up a crazy mixed-up kid with a switch-knife in my hand. I'm still surprised at how normally I grew up. But my father going broke was an invaluable lesson. Until that point I'd been terribly spoiled; now I learned life wasn't all a bed of roses. If he hadn't gone broke, I would certainly be a bigger bastard today and I wouldn't have been much of a racing driver.

The old man was colourful and strange; he was a character. If there was racing at Southport, he took his mechanics up there, he took their wives and girlfriends, he took any chum he met on the street, paying for everyone and everything. They still call him the Last of the Big Spenders, and he used money as though it were going out of fashion. He was just a player. A player as wide as he was tall. Very solid. He lived on a diet of

13

daily excitement and it did him in: with strokes and heart attacks and dreadful blood pressure. He was just fifty-one.

I don't think he could help himself. He drank a bottle of scotch a day. Then it was three-hour lunches and back at work for an hour and knock off for dinner. I was an obnoxious little bastard as a kid, a big-headed little shit: so people keep reminding me. When he was in the money, I was going to a flossy public school, driving an MG at sixteen, living in a nice house, going to Surfers Paradise for my holidays and the son of a famous man. A prescription for disaster. Next minute, no MG, no Surfers Paradise and three-quarters of the old man's friends have vanished: owing him money. Now I've seen both sides of the coin. His going broke dragged me down to earth; it taught me things can go wrong as well as right; and to be kind to people on the way up because you may meet them on the way down. Mainly, it taught me not to worry about what other people are doing or thinking: my job is to look after me and mine.

The old man also taught me manners come cheap. They cost nothing. If a man is a sweeper, say thank you and don't take him for granted. Please and thank you come cheap and they only take .2 of a second. I've tried to do that all my life: not to be arrogant and to treat people all the same way.

A.J. tells the story of his father discovering him in the back seat of the family car with an 'older woman' who seduced him at one of his father's parties. Father looked in the door, took in the predicament and apologized, saying, 'It seems my son is growing up.' It seems to have been an easy house.

My father outweighed my mother, his shadow sat on her, but there is a lot of my mother in me. She's from Irish stock, my grandfather's name being Paddy O'Brien, and you don't get more Irish than that. Whereas my father is Welsh. The pair of them met young and divorced when I was something like twelve. The divorce disappointed me. Looking back, it seems inevitable – there was always plenty of aggro in the house – but when you're a kid, nothing seems inevitable. I wasn't asked what I wanted, but I probably would have chosen to stay with my father. It was my mother who said I should; she was very sensible about it. My father could offer me things she couldn't. Mine wasn't a sitting-down-and-explaining sort of family. Nobody talked about the whys and wherefores back then and no one's talked about it since. No use.

I know what happened. The old man was a player and my mother would catch him out from time to time and there'd be a donnybrook. My mother was a volatile red-head: she'd say the wrong thing at the wrong time to my old man and he'd give her a whack. With that we'd be off on that week's little drama. My old man must have been a terrible man to live with and she wasn't the sort who says 'Yes dear,' and then turns a blind eye.

The divorce turned me into an independent and self-reliant kid. Nannies and housekeepers couldn't keep the padlocks on; my father wasn't around that much and I had the best sort of early training in conning everyone in sight.

If the reader will retain this vignette of family life, he will understand, later, why A.J., like many drivers, finds the Formula One family – and, more particularly, his own team – something like a substitute for the regularity, authority, security and consistency missing in childhood and youth. The point does not deserve to be laboured, but the racing urge is a very special urge; it is such a total declaration of ego that it has to imply a rejection of family authority. Young men set out to race; in A.J.'s case, his career was fostered by his father, but this is rare enough. Quite sensibly, like most of us, parents are not mad keen on the risks involved.

I went to a school called Xavier, a Catholic public school. I went to the Junior School first, Burge Hall, which is where you wear short trousers; and then it was up to Xavier where you have the honour of wearing long trousers. The school was run by Jesuits. There were a few lay-teachers, but most teachers were priests and they don't piss about. They've been strict with themselves and they're strict with you; the strap comes out at the slightest pretext.

We sat through religious instruction every day; we had to do our homework and learn our catechism, for we'd be questioned on it the next day. It contributed to my becoming an agnostic.

Father Brown ran the class with an iron rod. I was still a kid, but I can remember saying to myself: Hang on a minute, here's Father Brown, God's representative on earth, asking me, 'Jones, why is Jesus kind and gentle?' I remember Jones not knowing and then having the shit thrashed out of him by God's representative on earth for not knowing why Jesus was kind and gentle.

Like my mother, I have a keen nose for hypocrisy. I thought that one through and lost my faith. Not that it was ever very strong, being marked by lots of doubts and very little conviction. The brainwashing I had then, however, persists: I still cross myself when I see a funeral, I call on God when I get into trouble and I've even been known to say a prayer. Belief and desire have nothing to do with it: it was bashed into me.

Most drivers start their careers young: even if they don't make it into Formula One all that quickly. The kid who spends his leisure hours in a go-kart isn't going to be all that strong on history and mathematics. But drivers come in all sizes and shapes: mentally, too. Their education and general culture is in direct proportion to how much loot Daddy had. A.J., like James Hunt or Niki Lauda, was the product of prosperity. However relative that term is.

I was certainly no scholar. I thought I was far too good and clever to worry about sitting down and learning anything. How the hell, I thought, was Latin going to help me buy and sell or race motor cars? Which of course Latin and everything else does, in a roundabout way. But when you're Mr Smart aged thirteen, you don't think about education or getting help from anyone. My objectives as a child were strictly those of the day I was living in; tomorrow didn't exist.

I lived with my old man because he had the power and the money, but in fact as he was off racing or making money, I really lived with a succession of nannies and had the run of the house. I'd lock myself in my room and watch telly, stuff myself with chocolates or sneak out the window and run amok: there wasn't anyone around checking up on me. But I conned the nannies into thinking I'd spent the last two hours in my room studying. They'd swallow it and tell my old man what a good boy I'd been, and he'd be pleased and say, 'Good boy, Alan.' I knew the world was a con; it never bothered me to abuse their confidence.

But my home life didn't exactly propel me into scholarship. Maybe if I'd lived in a more normal, happy or typical household, and if my old man had taken a greater interest in me, I might have applied myself. But his interest was limited to my going to a good school and getting decent marks: he didn't care to know how or to police the fact.

Still I think of it as valuable. My son Christian will go to Xavier like me. Where I go, he should go. It's a good school, strong on sports, strong on the right kind of people. My old man was strong on the right sort of people. Maybe you don't agree with everything that's going on at school, he would say, but mark my words, at a good school you mix with the right people and you'll be able to do business with them when you're grown up. It sounds awful. When you're thirteen, that instruction doesn't mean much, but at thirty-four I understand it. Little Johnny Smith grows up and he's going to do business with his old mate Alan. It's never too early to learn the lessons money gives.

The childhood of a motor racing driver: training in getting what you want.

You can verify it in the careers of almost all racing drivers: almost without exception, they are all obsessed by machines and movement. That is why motor racing is in many ways not only the one sport which has developed exclusively in the Twentieth Century, but also the sport that best expresses the image of our times. Movement and machinery, and the individual freedom they have granted – of displacement, and shifts in our cultural perspectives – play a huge part in all our lives. The car is move-ment individualized: no dependencies, no schedules, no limita-tion. Get into it and you're off. A sub-branch of this overwhelming freedom is our worship of speed. The car not only offers freedom, it offers a chance at competition. One machine is better than another: faster, more beautiful, more comfortable, richer. . . . Track the childhoods of drivers and you'll find they'll do any-

17

thing to get into a machine and drive it: any machine. And the machine exists to be urged to ever greater speed.

I had something which other kids didn't have. The whole idea of racing, which was my chosen goal, was hereditary in me: because my father was a racing driver and because Stan Jones was known to be good. That meant I grew up with his mates and his mates' sons, and every last one of them was going to go racing, too: which they invariably didn't. But for me, there was this great big billboard in my mind that said, I've got to do it.

I started out in billy-cart racing, which is like the American Soap Box Derby. It consists of a great big hill and yourself on top. When the starter lets down the gate, you roll downhill. You can get up to 30 or 40 m.p.h. on the right hill and the one who got to the finish quickest won. I must have been about seven when I started and, typically, the old man went out and bought a special billy-cart built for Cotty's soft drinks, and I did that for about three years, winning my share. Even back then I wanted desperately to win and the old man would have been mortified if I hadn't. It wasn't that he pushed me into racing or pushed me once I went into it. He was the sort who would abuse the hell out of me if I did something wrong but would never compliment me if I did well: as though doing well were just expected of me.

After billy-carts, like most other drivers, I went into go-karts. I won the Australian championship when I was something like fifteen.

A go-kart, and we have all seen them, is a little boy's car. It's rather like the strange American habit of putting little kids into grown-up clothes, so the girls in their perms look like grandmas and the boys are premature Rotarians. It's a juvenile version of a grown-up sport: a rear-mounted engine, a basic chassis with just enough room for a boy's body, a track marked out with rubber tyres and – now – a recognized world championship. In this sport, there's no such thing as competing too young.

Then when I was sixteen and the old man was going into business without any money, we decided to buy this Mini from a repossession yard. Literally, the engine and the gears were in the boot, but the old man in his ignorance and his desire to please said, 'Take this down to Brian Sampson at Motor Improvements and get him to do it up.' In his mind, he was still living in his old Maserati days and he was thinking how a Mini couldn't cost more than a few bob to have fixed. Brian was told all we wanted was just the best under 1000 cc car in Australia and that's what we got. Only when the old man started getting the bills, he screamed: quite rightly he said it would have been cheaper to build a house.

There is nothing mechanical that can't be raced. At the top of the sport is Formula One, but there is no end to the lower levels. And most drivers will tell you that there's not all that much difference in the racing style or the competition; it can be as intense in a Mini or any of the other production-car categories – Renault, Volkswagen, Alfa, etc. – as in the multi-million-dollar top of the sport.

I had my first real car race in that Mini. It was at the Geelong Sprint, which is a standing quarter or half-mile race: two cars racing against each other with just one curve. I won that, because you don't have to be too clever to go fast in a straight line. I also did a few hillclimbs in that Mini and won them. With that under my belt, I managed to persuade the old man to lend me one of his Cooper-Climaxes, a 2.2 litre car. I dragged it out of the garage, checked the wheel-bearings and made sure everything was reasonably okay and entered it for a picnic meeting at Calder.

It was a nice friendly scene, like most lesser meets. The oil companies like BP, Shell and Castrol have their tents up and every driver has a contract, even if it's only worth ten quid and some oil; but that made us contracted drivers and that's a step up from the bottom. All you had to do was put a badge on your overalls and on the car and after the race pick up a steak sandwich from them and a beer. In the mornings there would be sprints and road-races in the afternoon. I entered the Cooper in everything and the little Mini, too. I blew everybody into the

19

weeds in the Cooper: there weren't that many kids at the meeting with a Cooper Climax!

The standard of preparation, and even the racing, was serious; at least I took it seriously. Going up the night before and staying in a real motel! It was all very professional and I felt I was on the way up; also I was living up to what was expected of me – I was Stan Jones' boy and I was expected to win. But when I look back on those days, I'm amazed. I didn't have any proper driving goggles, so I wore sunglasses. Now I think, Alan my boy, if you'd got a stone through those glasses, you'd be history!

Two themes: preparation, how cars are made to be good, and the quality of the car that's raced. A.J.'s old man had Coopers and Maseratis in his garage. Coopers were Jack Brabham's cars and swept the Formula One scene in the late fifties and early sixties; the Maseratis were the great cars of five years earlier. Technically A.J., by racing that Cooper in Australia, had made the fastest transition in motor-racing history: from saloon racing in his Mini to a Formula One drive in his Dad's Cooper, all within eight months.

Five years later, when he has come to England with those fifty quid in his pocket, his weight is listed as twelve stone, or 168 pounds. His hair is black, his eyes brown, and his blood-group, all-important in the sport, is listed as ARH positive. His likes – still on the letterhead of World Wide Sports Promotions – are listed as water-skiing, darts, squash, pop music, Natalie Wood and Italian food. It's the sort of simple-minded fact-sheet that you could produce on almost any racing driver: if anything, more typically middle-of-the-road and conventional. But A.J.'s rise was anything but typical. The body filled out, the man filled out, even the mind filled out.

In the fifties, the mecca of the racing driver would have been Italy, the cherished dream to drive for Ferrari, Alfa or Maserati. By the sixties, the scale had shifted entirely, and England had become what it was to remain until very recently: the hub of the sport. Like many a young man before and since, A.J. came to England. To seek glory. And, as he explains, with something of a shove in his back.

There I was, the son and heir, living well and going to inherit the business. Only it just didn't work out that way. The old man went bust and I suppose he didn't want me to face the embarrassment, the come-down in the world and the bailiffs around the childhood home, so he packed me off to England. I was all of twenty, having spent four years working in the old man's business in all sorts of capacities – it was called 'learning the business from the ground up' – and now I was shipped off. The old man was going to fiddle it through the business and send me so much a month every month, but things got so tight for him that he couldn't do it, and all I had was that fifty quid, so I had to make my own way. Very instructive it was, too.

I met up with my old chum Brian Maguire in England. We'd both done the mother-country tourist trip back in 1966 and Brian had stayed on when I went back to Australia to go into business with my Dad.

We moved in together and, as the first need was money, we started out in business together. Mini-vans were what we went into: Mini-vans for Aussies. You could buy them cheap and sell them not quite so cheap and turn over forty or fifty quid on a good day. Where we lived was determined by business. It had to be a basement flat with lots of parking room around it: all so that the landlord wouldn't know what we were up to. It also had to be near a station, because Aussies in London knew where Earls Court was but not much else; the rest was like Darkest Africa to them, and you had to be able to pinpoint an underground and say, you come out of the station and turn right. We were lucky. The street we were on backed onto a railway line so that when we had our vans bumper to bumper on the street we didn't have to bother about Mrs Houseproud coming out in her curlers and telling us our vans were lowering the tone of the neighbourhood.

We kept that up for a year and made enough to keep the wolf from the door. And also to buy my first car: a Formula Ford single-seater, in which I did a few practice sessions until Brian wrote it off. We didn't waste it, mind you: we took all the pieces, the engine, the chassis, the wheels, the gearbox and put it all together again. Like Humpty-Dumpty. The flat looked like a garage.

There begins, early, this intimacy between man and machine, the one literally living with the other, that marks the driver's career. They are curiously dependent upon each other, these two: the man without a machine is helpless, the machine without a driver is at a standstill. The more they marry, the deeper their intimacy, the better the results for both.

Both Brian and I were into motor racing. Well into it. All we lacked was a car, and I knew I just had to have a racing car and the opportunity to go out and do my thing. There's a way to go about getting into racing; it doesn't depend strictly on yourself. You have to know the trade people, because they supply you and can perhaps sponsor you; you have to know the circuits, because that's where you're going to drive; and, above all, you have to drive, because that's why you exist.

To get a car, we needed more money. So we took a step up from Mini-vans and went into the caravan business, buying up the old Bedfords with the windows in their sides and the hard wooden seats. We would put a little primus stove inside and a couple of rolled-up sleeping bags and sell them to Assies to do the Grand Tour of Europe in. We pasted the back windows with stickers as though the vans had already been everywhere there was to go, and when people answered the ads we'd sell them the big trip. If you sold the fresh air and the beautiful castles of Germany, the history of France, and the romance of Italy hard enough, they wouldn't look too closely at the vans. It was so easy, we thought the business would last forever. Which it might have, if we'd taken it the least little bit seriously.

But by then I'd bought a Lotus 41, a Formula Three single-seater, and my first real racing car. It was two years old, but brand new. I stripped the whole car down, I had the chassis sand-blasted and the paintwork enamelled. I made it into a bloody beauty, without realizing that it isn't beauty that wins races but a car in working order. And I'd neglected to check that they'd taken all the sand out after they'd done the face-lift. I had a gorgeous little car, all gassed up and doing nicely, only I threw six engine bearings in a row. An auspicious beginning.

Finally, we worked out why the bearings were going and I devised my little scheme. I would make my Lotus fit Australian

Formula Two specifications, take it back home, flog it and come back to go Formula Three racing. That was the plan, anyway.

Formula Three and Formula Two are simply lesser versions of single-seater formula racing, with smaller engines, smaller chassis and less elaborate safety and technical requirements. At current prices, a Formula Three drive might cost £75,000, a Formula Two twice that. A Formula One car equals, if available, and at its minimum cost, something like four to five times a Formula Three car. But the art of driving can – indeed, must – be learned in the lesser formulae.

But any racing car is a large investment. And, as A.J. was soon to find out, when all your money is tied up in one car and that gets into a shunt, your future becomes more problematical. In Formula One, with all its sponsorship, its works-produced cars, its huge investment, the average team might use as many as ten to sixteen cars a year, depending on the skill and reliability of the team's drivers. But in Formula Three, a written-off car is a total disaster. It's back to square one.

One day I was out at Brands Hatch testing. Everything was going sweetly and I was putting in respectable, if not brilliant, times. Good enough, anyway, since I was new to my car, new to the sport and a relative newcomer to the circuit. It was a Wednesday and Brands Hatch was a muddle. Open practice and the circuit filled with every kind of car under the sun: Formula Fords and whatnot sprayed all over the track. The paddock was on the left-hand side of the circuit and ahead of me there was this bloke driving away: no problems, I'll pass him nice and easy on the right. Except that he suddenly decided that he would turn into the pits. I was inexperienced. At the time, I thought the main thing was to miss him: so I went round him – right round him, winding up off the track, in the grass with the Lotus a complete write-off. End of big sale in Australia. End of Formula Three car to be bought when I came back. End of A.J.'s career.

I wasn't married to Beverly back then – we were in one of our off-and-on periods of big fights and even bigger getting-back-togethers – but being a good, loyal girl, she'd decided to come out to Brands to see her man taking his car out. She arrived just in time to hear this big bang and see me lying in the grass and swearing my head off about how I was going to kill the bastard that cut across me. It wasn't just the anger. There was also the sadness. There was my Lotus, all lovely, all re-sprayed, a mess in the grass, just like me.

Finally they got an ambulance to me and took me off to hospital. It was my first shunt and the hospital must have been built in the Boer War. They took me into Casualty, and there was this lady doctor standing over me, screaming. I should stop doing this criminal thing, she said. I could sympathize; she'd had another driver in the week before and she didn't want a bloody mess in her clean cubicle after last week. So she went on yelling at me about didn't I know what would happen to me if I persisted in my fatal course? Finally, I said to her politely, 'I'll tell you what, Madam, you get on with your job and I'll get on with mine.' By then, you understand, with a broken leg, I wasn't feeling altogether polite.

Reluctantly, she took out a pair of scissors and was about to go to work on my brand new Nomex overalls. It was my turn to yell at her: she wasn't going to snip at my valuable equipment. She desisted, helped me up on to the operating table and said she wouldn't be long. I lay there with my leg hurting like hell for some ten minutes listening to the rattle of tea cups in the next room. Finally, she came back and they put plaster on my leg. The week after, I went to have it checked in Chiswick and they said, as all doctors love to say, that they'd done it all wrong the first time. So they did it again. All wrong. Which is why, even now, ten years later, it still hurts me sometimes, and why I don't have all that much faith in doctors and hospitals.

Unlike all the other formulas, Formula One actually provides quite superior and rapid medical treatment for drivers. And has to, injuries being sufficiently frequent. In 1980, a typical year, A.J.'s old team-mate Clay Regazzoni had a major shunt which left him paralyzed from the waist down. The Long Beach medical unit had all the facilities for cardiac surgery, but could not do much for Clay. Later in the year, Renault driver Jean-Pierre Jabouille broke both his legs, jammed against the floor of the cockpit at high speed, and is only just, six months later, recovering the use of his legs. Such accidents are a routine part of the sport. Like the risk of death, they are taken for granted. A.J.'s laconic tone, the ability to make fun of his own pain, is par for the course.

After that shunt at Brands, there was nothing left of the Lotus but the engine, and I sold that. The shunt didn't deter me; I was no sooner up and about than I started looking for another car to race. I found a Brabham BT 28, raced it on borrowed tyres and won. I followed that up with a few Formula Three races in which I hardly set the world on fire. This was when opportunity seemed to knock at the door and Promoto entered my life. Re-entering it was my father, who had had enough of creditors and heart attacks in Australia and came over to live with me in England.

Promoto was a company which, as its name implies, promoted you; in fact, they all but guaranteed to make you a Formula One driver overnight. I was deeply suspicious, but God knows I needed promotion; I seemed to be getting nowhere fast. What clinched the deal for me was when I heard that my friend Brian was in charge of picking the drivers to do some Formula Three racing in Brazil. I said I would join Promoto if they picked me to go to Brazil. I handed over three hundred and fifty quid and, guess what? Brian picked me to go to Brazil.

Going places. Racing is an unfixed abode. There is a race to be faced every second week for most of nine months in the year. The normal habitat of the driver is an hotel room, and year after year, drivers will stay in the same hotels in the same places, seeing the same people and doing the same thing. Thus exotic places like Rio de Janeiro or South Africa will fade into their respective Sheraton or Hilton hotels, one swimming pool will become indistinguishable from another. The countries themselves, except for a few outlying restaurants, will remain terra incognita. The French driver Jacques Laffite will go fishing in the Andes; Jochen Mass, the German veteran, has friends he stays with all over the world and a boat to hide on between races, but for most drivers, the world of travel is bounded by four walls hung with

*mediocre prints, a bathroom, a coffee shop downstairs and a
restaurant within easy walking or driving distance.*

*Thus all the hoopla of the jet-set is really ash in their mouths.
Except in matters of diet – and even then, the majority are
steak-and-potatoes men – they do not live in different countries;
there are just better places and worse places. Joint Number One
on the hate-list used to be Belgium and Sweden. Because of the
remoteness of the circuits and the uncivilized surroundings.
There are fewer girls, no handy tennis courts and swimming
pools, languages they don't understand and, often, rainy weather.
Monaco is a favourite because drivers love to study poseurs and
groupies and quite enjoy the parties in the yachts tied up in
Rainier's back garden; Italy is liked for its vivacity, Long Beach
for being in California, Kyalami in South Africa because of its
leisurely pace.*

*But that first step the young driver makes into foreign parts,
shedding his sheltered existence and his adolescence, is usually
a profound culture shock.*

I was about twenty-four when I hit Brazil and I'd never been
anywhere much except England. It seemed somehow miraculous
to find myself in a place that was so profoundly different. All I
wanted to do when we landed, was hit the town. I'd brought my
Dad with me and Jim, my mechanic, and while Dad slept off
the trip in our hotel, Jim and I went out for a walk. I think we
knew what we were looking for. Fortunately, or unfortunately,
our hotel was just up the road from a night-club, and of course
we had to venture into it.

Well, we no sooner sat down at a table and ordered up a few
beers when there were half-a-dozen birds sitting down all round
us, groping under the table and grabbing us. As long as you
drink, the girls are there to keep you happy. And not just dogs,
either: the women of Brazil are beautiful. I'd never struck anything like this in my life and I turned to Jim and said, how
long's this been going on? and why have I been missing out? It
was my very first taste of the international glamour and I fell
for it. It wasn't until I was a lot older and more experienced –
and even then, not always – that I realized the pitfalls of the

glamour. I have the only really bad race of my career to remind me where I learned the lesson.

Before we left for Brazil, I thought to myself that I'd better take those Formula Three races down there seriously. I suppose I was evolving, slowly. Brazil was, after all, my first major professional racing: not just being in a motel the night before but travelling half-way across the world for three races. I bought myself a year-old super engine that was going to be my *pièce de résistance*, the screamer I'd keep in the wings. I wanted desperately to do the right thing. I wasn't brilliant in the first two races at Interlagos in Sao Paulo; the screamer packed up. But when we went down to Porto Alegre for the third race, Jim and I nodded knowingly at each other and we said, 'Okay, let's put the wings on for this one'; I'd never driven a car with wings on before.

Wings, front and rear, stabilize the car and prevent it from lifting off the track at speed. They are also fragile members and their sudden loss can cause disaster.

I was about fifth quickest in practice, and afterwards Dave Walker, a fellow Australian, came up to me in the pits asking me how things were going. I said very nicely thank you; I was quite pleased with myself and, I might add, with the friendly attention of a real big-time racing driver like Dave. 'Well,' he said, laconically, 'I think you could do a whole lot better if you put your front wing on the right way, because you've got it on back to front!' With that little bit of exact science under my belt, I managed to get myself on the front row with Walker and everybody was tickled to death and running about as if they didn't know what had happened. I didn't know myself.

We were all celebrating our triumph when Peter Warr came round to our garage and started to examine my wings because I was as fast as his driver, Dave Walker. Peter figured that had to be because my car was bent. He sniffed around, took out his tape measure, announced that I was a centimetre too wide and he was going to protest the grid position. My old man didn't take kindly to any of this. In fact, though his speech wasn't all that clear by then, his walking stick made his point for him.

27

The old man chased Peter right out of our garage and only narrowly missed cracking his skull. Which wasn't from lack of effort. We sawed a centimetre off, I ran sixth in the race until my gear box gave out and that was my big Brazilian opportunity.

The exact sizes of engines, chassis, wheels and overall dimensions are controlled by the elaborate rules which govern each formula. Peter Warr, who was later to work with Lotus for many years, was well within his rights. In the year in which James Hunt was to win the World Championship, his results at the Spanish Grand Prix were annulled because of a surplus millimetre or two. The regulations exist, in fact, only to be reinterpreted. Each constructor does his best to get around them or to invent some new dodge – in motor racing talk, a 'tweak' – that the regulations have not foreseen.

The regulations are vital, of course, because of the huge investments in developing new engineering technology. The greater the investment, the more important it is that the rules be known in advance and be relatively stable; but, as motor racing is a constantly evolving sport, particularly on the technical side, there is no handy way of suppressing innovation. Consequently, there are always arguments and protests about unfair advantage being taken. Most of the time, these arguments are fought out and resolved within the family of constructors, but within that family, as throughout the sport, competition is fierce and one-upmanship the name of the game.

The next step was a 1600 cc Brabham we could make from a kit, thus turning the old BT 28 into a BT 28/35. Our problem was that we were new boys in racing, and new boys can't expect to get the best of anything. We had no real money: how were we to get our hands on a first-class engine? I thought of George Robinson. Everybody needs someone like George Robinson: someone who backs you and sticks by you. George let us have an engine, and in the very first race we ran, we were the only people around with a proper Formula Three engine and we fronted it all over the field.

That cost us a few more altercations. Once again our garage

was full of bods and sods saying our engine must be bent or we couldn't get that much power; but the engine was tested and it was all in order. So everyone started asking George for his engines, but George stuck to his word: he continued to give us good engines, better engines than he gave to people who came in later with cash in hand.

We are now in the world of Formula Three, where the drivers come basically in two sorts: rich kids with rich daddies and less-rich kids with ambitions and a gift for the con. As A.J. says, much of motor racing goes on before you ever get in a car. A concert pianist can do his five-finger exercises on his lap in an aeroplane; any church hall will have a piano. Not so in motor racing. There you need a car.

But Formula Three is still a friendlier world than Formula One. The transporters, the campers, the motor-homes are the same, just less lavish. The sponsors are around, but in for less. Often they are local sponsors: a garage, a travel firm, shoe manu- facturers, most of them enthusiasts in their own right. The look – of friendly mechanics, sweating wives, company reps and middle-men – is roughly the same: but the ties are not by Pierre Cardin, the shoes from Gucci or the catering from Roger Vergé. The Formula Three paddock is more often a grubby, muddy field without water-tanks or laid-on mains electricity; teams make do with flasks of coffee and biscuits. Despite the difference in scale, one rule remains the same whatever the formula: everyone de- pends on the grace and favour of someone else – the man who can provide a decent set of tyres, who can supply oil on a deal, a gear-box, bail them out in a crisis. Drivers depend on cars and sponsors, sponsors on the press and coverage, mechanics on their employers or friends, teams on their suppliers, the suppliers on customers.

The problem is that the risks are no less in this nether world. If anything, they are greater, for the drivers are more inexperi- enced, time and fate have not weeded out the wild men, the cars are less strong, not so thoroughly tested nor that carefully pre- pared. There's no real margin for error: the cars, the crowds, the money are smaller, the fields larger, the circuits less secure. No medical helicopters dance attendance on the unlucky; the track marshalls are more widely scattered. And with all that, a driver has to shine; he must be not only good and quick, but also have attention paid to him.

Therein lies the con. How to put yourself forward, how to be noticed. And, to get noticed, drivers in Formula Three will do almost anything. They will try that much harder, attempt the more spectacular move. And the failure rate is correspondingly higher: including a high proportion of those who entered the sport thinking they had what the sport demands in the way of skills or bravery, and who found themselves wanting. Formula Three is as much a graveyard as it is a testing- and forcing-ground for successful drivers.

The failures, the cock-ups, the near-misses, the hairy shunts all make for good stories, and most drivers one has known in Formula One have a certain nostalgia for their days in Formula Three. Akin to that feeling old-time Formula One drivers have, who tell you about the Golden Age back when they were driving, and men were men and money didn't matter.

Formula Three is like the boyhood of the professional driver; it's that period when he has to prove he's a man by sniping at authority, walking off with a rival's sponsor or his bird. But like all boyhoods, it's also the time when a driver learns his trade. Not merely the driving skills, which depend to some extent on his natural talent, but all the other aspects of the sport on which the driver survives. For the top of the sport is a rich man's club into which you have to claw your way. And down at these lower levels most drivers spend from one to three or four years. A hard apprenticeship.

Meanwhile, ordinary life continued. There was still the daily bread to be earned. This was now 1971, which was going to be my big year in Formula Three. Big is a relative word. Certainly, we had big ideas, Brian and I; I sometimes think it was an infection I caught from my old man.

We set up the world's first, last and only all-Australian racing team. It was called AIRO, for Australian International Racing Organization, and it was frightfully, frightfully smart. We had our transporter and our cars and they were all clean and gleaming and painted orange. Our gear was good and we stood there nicely lined up having our pictures taken, all of us grinning as though we earned the world. You should never advertize prosperity, especially when you're not prosperous. People looked at our team and whistled. We looked so good everyone thought we were in sponsors up to our armpits. And where were the money men we were looking for who would sidle up to us and whisper, Could you fellows use a little money? Nowhere, is the answer. But it wasn't that bad a season in Formula Three: I won a few races and finished decently in the championship. High enough to get myself noticed a bit, I thought. That was where I was wrong.

For all but a few drivers at the top of the profession – as A.J. is now, commanding almost any fee he wants from a team that might want him – the winter close season is a period of discontent. More than most sports, motor racing is fraught with insecurities. Many are called and few chosen and this is but one of the reasons for the inconsistency of work. For, to be a works driver, many financial conditions must be satisfied.

It starts at the bottom, where a new driver might have to pay a constructor for his seat in that constructor's car. Almost all teams have had rent-a-drivers, and the price can be very high. Sums of up to a million a season have been laid out just to be able to participate. Sometimes a rented driver makes good: the next year he may race at par, or even earn a little bread. Above the rent-a-driver stands the promising beginner: good enough for a crack at a drive, he's not good enough, or proven enough, to command much of a retainer. In his first year in Formula One, a beginning driver, with some years of Formula Three and probably a season or two in Formula Two as well, might command between $25,000 and $100,000 U.S.; and, after a more or less successful season, a few points earned, a few good results, a large number of finishes, showing consistency, he might command up to $200,000.

The trouble, as with most scales, is that there are ways of falling down as well as rising up. Many drivers live to see their retainers shrink as their reputations, and their results, dwindle. It is in middle career that you see most drivers shifting from

31

team to team in a vain attempt to bolster their reputations or their incomes.

Winter means incertitude. Those not hired as the previous year's season comes to an end, suffer the anxiety of a long wait. Many never make it into the next year, who were much hailed when they arrived on the scene.

The winter after my first full Formula Three season was like every other winter I've known until I joined Frank Williams: cold, long and unsettling. I spent it by the telephone waiting for it to ring and wondering why it all wasn't happening. I thought I'd done well enough to be picked up by some team for a works drive, but it was as though once the season was over, I faded from sight.

Those are hard times for a driver. Even bitter times, especially at the beginning of your career, when you're bound to rate yourself higher than anyone else is likely to. I'd turn up at tracks, I'd call people up, I'd let it be known I was available, but the only real thing that happened that winter was a chance to test for March at Silverstone.

March, Tyrrell, Lotus, Brabham: the names belong to constructors. Constructors are those who make cars for racing. They may also be involved in manufacturing production cars, as Lotus is, or Ferrari, Renault and Alfa, but their heart is in racing. In those days, March, formed from the design brains of Robin Herd and the selling energy of Max Mosley, was a struggling beginner in the constructor's world, but doing well from the start. In Formula One, it never enjoyed huge success, even though many of the world's best drivers drove for them at one time or another, but in Formula Two, it was a power and remains one. Thus, a chance for A.J. to test in a March was a big event.

They were beautiful, simple, agile little cars. The only trouble with them was that I couldn't afford one. I couldn't really afford to go out and drive ten-tenths in one, in case I smashed it up. But, being me and being a heedless bastard, I didn't think of that. It was a sort of 'open day' to look over the new March cars and Robin had invited me up. I was surrounded, literally, by rich kids who'd driven up in their brand-new Porsches and who had sponsorship cheques dripping from the back pockets of their Eyetie trousers and were whipping around photos of their little pad in Surrey they'd hired at some exorbitant price for the 'season'. It was enough to make anyone sick, these kids walking in and ordering brand new cars, brand new engines and then saying, 'Christ! I nearly forgot a transporter! Can you tell me where I can find a new transporter?'

I knew half of them couldn't drive out of sight on a dark night, and I couldn't help the anger and the envy. Now I realize that they thought pretty much as I thought: that they were going to go out and race and brain everybody in sight. Because I don't think many people go into motor racing *knowing* they can't drive and will never make it; some just take longer than others to get that unhappy message. And among them are probably some with huge potential who drop out at the slightest little set-back: life hasn't hardened them up enough.

The money is just around. It's the natural climate of the sport, as smog is to Los Angeles. Some drivers, at the top, have a lot of it, but it permeates down the field. The constructors, despite their perpetual worries about financing, all have a sufficiency; or, of course, play the old con game, and live as though they do. Sponsors, by definition, have it: they do not have to pay their own entertainment bills. All the handsome attaché cases one sees in the first-class lounges of airplanes as drivers and constructors move from circuit to circuit, are well-stocked with international currencies and plastic. After all, money is the Number One incentive for many; it is compensation for the risks.

And money produces its hangers-on and parasites. They provide the distraction and the artificial glamour that surrounds the sport like a cocoon. To the point where, for some, this has become the real reason for their racing. It is something they could no longer live without: the recognition, the availability of services, the air-conditioned existence.

I happen not to think that's what the sport is about, and I've never liked that aspect of it. It's not about glamour and games. In fact, I've despised a number of the characters I've seen around in the sport who feel that way. But not always. Like everyone else, I'm ambivalent about them, and sometimes I recognize it's good that there are such people. It's good for the sport's image. It is that part of our lives the public chooses to identify with: our life-style, our freedom to drive a car as fast as we can. It's part envy.

The silk scarves and the blondes on the arm are the raw meat you feed to an animal: namely, the public. The public gobbles it up. So how can I resent these people? They are our sacrificial lambs. They don't bother me any more: unless of course they're also quick and a threat to me. They make up the numbers and provide the spice; they satisfy those who don't understand the sport, the surface people, who outnumber the rest. I laugh at them, stick them up on a shelf, label them and forget about them. But when I started racing, they were a source of constant frustration.

I have never looked on my racing career as a means to go cocktail partying or meeting people or being chic. Perhaps a little less so today, but my life has always been lived on a day-to-day basis, with me unable to see anything further than the next race, nothing having meaning except a competitive car and beating people and proving them wrong.

The people I care about are those in my profession, and even there, mainly in the very narrow circle made up of the people I race with: my car, my mechanics, my team. If they're happy, I'm happy, because I race for an inner circle. But that's now. Back then, in Formula Three, I raced for myself. It was a form of individual combat. I actually resented the other people who were doing what I was doing, because they were in my way. Those were simpler-minded days: my philosophy of driving was to get into anything I could and go as fast as I could, and if I smashed a car up, well, I'd think about paying for it later.

So on that day at Silverstone, I blew all the rich kids off the circuit and put in a time damn close to Roger Williamson's, who was March's great white hope. That made a few eyes pop. Enough, anyway, to get me invited back by March to do a few tests with just Williamson and myself, he being the big name and myself being the nobody. Which didn't prevent me from being quicker than he was. But it was a dead-end situation: I couldn't afford to pay March for a car and they didn't feel they could afford to pay me to drive for them. Yet a works drive is the first goal of every beginning driver, his badge of professionalism, the moment when he does what he wants to do, when someone is spending money on him instead of his spending money on them.

It was a come-down to have to spend so much of my time wheeling and dealing on the telephone and buying and selling caravans, yet the rent and the phone bill had to be paid. But in 1972, I got my GRD car: GRD lent me the chassis, the blessed George Robinson lent me the engine. I was supposed to return the chassis at the end of the season in the condition in which I had received it. I was meant to pay insurance and the rest, but of course I didn't: I couldn't afford the kind of insurance racing drivers have to carry and also I thought, 'Oh bugger! I'm not going to have a crash!'

George had faith in me; all he wanted was that I should drive the car and do well. But by then I was spending so much time testing and mucking about in racing cars that Brian Maguire and I split. I couldn't honestly keep up with the business side of it; also I didn't see any need to share the profits with someone else. So I rented a house in Ealing and started buying and selling caravans on my own. I put the GRD in the garage, brought my mechanic Jim Hardman in to work for me from 9 to 5, concentrating 100 per cent on the car, and I just put in longer hours, going out at night and flogging my caravans.

By the end of the year I had an overdraft I'm still proud of. It's no easy task for an Aussie without chattels, security or his own home to get into a bank for twelve grand; but I also helped out the bank manager's wife and I survived. I was, after all, at last a works driver. The last works Formula Three driver, I think, for after me it was all Brazilian millionaire kids over here with the ready.

Right from the start, I couldn't do anything with the car. It just wouldn't handle. Yet GRDs were the cars you were supposed to have. I knew it wasn't my fault, so I talked GRD into taking the car back, stripping it completely and rebuilding it from scratch. When they returned it to me, I went straight out and came in second in my very first race. From which I learned a lesson: it is very important to get your car right and no use driving ten-tenths unless you do, because you still won't get anywhere. Whereas, if you get it right, the car will do all the work and you'll get the results.

From the outside, the hierarchy of the formulae, Formula Three to Formula Two to Formula One, each stronger, quicker, safer, richer than the last, looks like a primrose path: you start at the bottom and work your way up the ladder, rung by rung. Every activity has its illusions and few indeed, in most walks of life, are those who start at the top. In motor racing, none. The truth is that in the lesser formulae, life can be a messy and precarious business. There are times when a driver's future seems assured, only for the cup to be smartly dashed from his lips.

True, the aces of Formula One speak nostalgically of their free-wheeling days in Formula Three, but for some of those, even, the memories are not unmixed with disappointments and travail. World Champions like Niki Lauda or James Hunt spent their early careers in endless accidents; Mario Andretti's motor racing ambitions were formed while he jockeyed cars in an Italian parking garage. Alan had his share of dry wells before he struck Arab oil.

A Scottish industrialist called Dennis Dobby proposed to enter the sport. Every year there are one or two like him: they have a little surplus money and they think motor racing ought to be fun. Dobby announced that he was going to sponsor three cars for GRD: a sports car for John Miles, a Formula Two car for Dave Walker and a Formula Three car for me. With much jollity and self-congratulation, we signed up. My first year was to be in Formula Three, my second in Formula Two and my third in Formula One! I signed the contract and thought, Well, this is it! I've done it at last!

I did my year in Formula Three. My car was kept at the factory, all I had to do was drive up in my road car and hop into the racer. Fantastic! Plenty of time to make spare cash during the week: all I had to do was go down to Snetterton once a week, sometimes twice, to test. After the uncertainties I'd been through, this looked like the real thing.

Unfortunately, as the year progressed, Dobby's Formula Two car wasn't all that competitive, and his sports car was even less so. Not unnaturally, as I was having good results and leading the European Formula Three championships, Dobby turned all his attention to Formula Three, ignoring his other cars and drivers. That didn't promise all that well for the future, for this isn't a sport you expect immediate results in.

The last race of the season was at Brands Hatch, and I needed to finish seventh or better to win the championship. I went out to practise in the morning, and my engine blew up and we were forced into the kind of situation I hate: a big, panic change of engine over lunch. Nothing should be done in a hurry in racing, except the drive itself; for everything else, you need calm. They got the engine in, just in time, and I gave it a quick try: the bloody thing wouldn't fire properly, or was running on one too few cylinders. I knew I was in for trouble.

I was on the front row when the race started, but with the engine misfiring, I dropped back and back with every lap of the race until I found myself in seventh place, which was as far back as I could allow myself to go if I wanted to win the championship – which I very badly did. Lying eighth was Larry Perkins, another Aussie, who wore glasses as thick as Coca Cola bottle-bottoms. As we went down into Hawthorn, Larry tried to pass me on the outside; I moved over to take up my line, and the next thing I know, we rub wheels and I see Larry's Brabham spinning down the straight. I wasted no sympathy on Larry. I just thought, 'Thank God for that, I'm still in seventh place and I should make it now.'

I expected to come around on the next lap and see ambulances all over the place, but when I came around, the track was clear: not a sign of Larry and I wondered where the hell he finished up, because he must have hit something. No such luck! Lo and behold, I looked in my mirror and there was this white Brabham coming back at me. 'Oh no! Don't! Please don't! Here I am with some seven laps to go, a buggered engine, and if only I can stay in seventh place, the championship is mine, but if he passes me, that's done it!'

Well, the engine grew progressively worse, he passed me, I finished eighth and lost the championship to Tony Brise by one point. Disappointed is not the word; I was shattered. I headed straight for the bar after the race and there I heard someone say Larry Perkins was going to enter a protest against me for dangerous driving. Larry at that stage was the new boy in Europe and he was writing for the newspapers back home about how Tim Schenken and other drivers whose boots, in my own personal opinion, he wasn't fit to clean were over the hill; he wrote how this was my third year in Formula Three and he didn't see me progressing much beyond this point. Well, he put in four years, and where's Larry now? You could say we never struck up a dear relationship.

Anyway, in the bar, when he walked in, I went up to him and said I'd heard he intended to protest me for dangerous driving. He answered that he hoped he would never have the displeasure of racing against me again: which he didn't, because he never made it in Formula One.

Three morals are contained in this little episode from A.J.'s early days at Brands Hatch. First, that no result is ever in the bag, for every driver is in the hands of the gods who control mechanical imperfections. The A.J. of those days, who sported tufty side-burns and wore a moon-like face of surprising innocence, was still burly and fit; and was not, any more than he is now, above a good bar-room brawl. His old man, he says, was likely to favour a fight over a fuck. Like father, like son. Secondly, the championship meant a good deal to A.J.: it was important not merely for the inner satisfaction of winning, and not merely for his ego, but because it should have led the way to further progress up the racing ladder.

The third moral to be drawn is that there are quarrels within the Family. When so many are at the trough, appetites and tempers are directly related, and there are no few altercations and fisticuffs on the track when one driver feels he's been dealt with unfairly by another. Master James Hunt was notorious for his temper. The sheer combative energy of the sport, the constant hype, the stress of keeping in front, all combine to create the occasional explosion.

What A.J. is objecting to about Perkins, who had no significant further career, is that he was an inferior, and it is a rule of the sport that inferiors yield to their betters. Even were that not so, most drivers who know they're good – and in their heart of hearts, most drivers make no real mistake on this subject – cannot believe that they can be beaten by their inferiors. The logic of the sport says that the best driver, if his car holds up, must win. Yet it has never been 100 per cent so. Neither Stirling Moss nor Ronnie Peterson, two of the quickest and most accomplished drivers the sport has ever seen, ever won a world championship. Or consider the New Zealander Chris Amon: fourteen seasons racing, six pole positions, 784 kilometers leading races and not even a Grand Prix win to his name. And not a driver who raced against him but knew he was good. Injustice, in short, is part of the game.

It was another of those winters. I had done obviously well in Formula Three, and during the season I had the usual expressions of interest: in fact I'd been courted. But this was just about the nastiest winter of them all. I no sooner got a drive teed up than it fell through. I had been looking forward to the next season's racing with GRD and my promised Formula Two drive. Of course that never materialized. I was told Dobby was pulling out of racing and so were GRD: I'd better go look for a drive for myself. I was used to it. Only in the last four seasons have I been able to relax over Christmas. Otherwise I haven't had my mind on the Xmas tree; I've had to think how I was going to keep my racing body and soul together.

Also, I had to protect my rear, in case the answer to all my winter questioning was that nothing was happening. The fact is, someone like myself has got to stick it out. I wasn't a playboy. I've never known playboys that were all that good. Niki Lauda was a wheeler and dealer and still is, but he lived in a basement flat in Earls Court and he didn't go around fronting it all over town. Like me, he took his racing seriously. It hardens your character that you have to wheel and deal. Playboys can go out and just buy what they want. But they don't generally make it. When the shit hits the fan they don't have to stick it out and they usually don't. If things don't go their way, they call it a day.

But I had to stick it out. For me, it was either throw in the towel and go back to Australia and become a car salesman or have enough strength and conviction to fight for what I wanted. I knew I was determined and I knew I would still be trying to get into Formula One at thirty-five or forty. It meant a whole lot of things to me to do so: proving people wrong about me, reaching my own goals, not wanting to go back to Australia a failure. That last especially. It isn't as though the whole Australian public were waiting with bated breath to see if I made it or not, but my friends sure were. And then, as I've said, my driving was hereditary.

I'd seen my old man in his disappointments. He said he'd made his decision not to race in Europe and he didn't regret it. Most of the time, I believe him. But sometimes I think that when my father stood there and said he wished he'd done Europe, which he said as often as he said he didn't regret not having done it, in his heart of hearts he knew he hadn't really wanted to race in Europe. Or not badly enough. So that maybe deep down he was glad he hadn't. I don't know.

My old man was distracted because he wanted to be distracted. He was distracted because he never had to answer to a boss or a sponsor; he was his own boss, he was his own sponsor. That makes it all different. If I were a trillionaire and had my own Formula One team, I'd be answerable to nobody: but probably I wouldn't have got as far as I have, for I'd have been too busy playing around. I haven't played around; I haven't had time to. I always knew I was only getting one crack at the big prize, which is Formula One, and I had to make the best of my own chance.

I didn't want to be like my old man. I wanted to be what I am. Which is: someone able to stand up at the bar, shrug my shoulders at anyone and say I don't have any laments or complaints. I was there, I did it, I'm satisfied. If I were in Timbuktoo draining swamps, I'd still have done it. Nobody can take that away from me. I chose to do it, I came over to Europe and did it and I never bought a ride in my life. I've done it all *my* way and that's important to me.

For I recognize that I'm an egotist's son, that I'm an egotist myself and that everyone I know in motor racing is no less of an egotist than I am. I race for the satisfaction of myself. I enjoy the accolades, but that's not what it's about for me.

When I began in Formula Three and I had my first works drive and the transporters rolled up, the motor home and all the gear, I thought, 'Christ! all this is here for me!' I was more worried about that fact than I was about the race. I thought, 'If I don't win, all this effort's going to have been wasted!' I had to force myself to think it through, to sit there and tell myself, 'Hang on a minute, all this stuff is here to go motor racing, and if you don't win, that's tough, but all you've got to give is your best.' Concentration is all. The old man was distracted. I wasn't going to be. Not if I could help it.

1974 was starting, I had nothing going for me and I was getting desperate. I went up to a race meeting at Silverstone and ran into Bev Bond, who told me he knew a man down Cirencester way who had a car and was looking for someone to drive it. I waited not a minute. I called him right up. He was one of these men who come on strong right away over the blower: bluff, straightforward. 'Look,' he said, 'I want you to know we're not mucking about here, we're going to do this properly!' He told me he had a Formula Atlantic March and a transporter and he'd barely hung up before I was down there.

The trouble is, you meet all sorts in this game. I pulled up in his street and there was this Nestlé chocolate van outside his place. Out of the back of it was poking something that looked like an open-wheeler. I knew I'd been put deep in it right away. The van was his transporter and that car inside like a slab of beef was going to be the great new challenge in the 1974 Atlantic series!

I weighed up the alternative, which was nothing, wasted no time over it, and said, 'All right, I'll drive for you, but first I've got to go and do a test drive at Snetterton.' He agreed, looking as though he were doing me all the favours. When we got down to the circuit we pulled the car out together, set it down on the ground and it was plain to see there wasn't one wheel pointing in the right direction. I tried to look very cool and business-like and I said the wheels being all awry was no problem; we could get that fixed. I would drive for him in the Martini International at Silverstone if he'd get his car fixed by March.

He took the car to March and they answered back smart-quick: the sensible thing for us to do was throw that car away like a used Kleenex and buy a new one, because we weren't going to get that one fixed up for less than five grand. So I talked to Robin Herd myself and I told him to forget the rest, just to get the wheels on straight and I'd have a go. I think that shows just how bad that winter was.

Meanwhile, Mr Nestlé Van was giving me a hard time about how I was test mad and asking for too much. I suppose he'd been brought up in the old school or flown Spitfires put together with chewing gum. But the whole scene with him wasn't looking that good. I remembered meeting Baron Beck at Brands the year before, and he'd offered to sponsor me in Formula Two. I called him again, with not a lot of money involved – enough to get the car on the track – and he agreed.

I took the car to Silverstone, I qualified about fifth quickest and Bev Bond was on pole (i.e., *having qualified fastest*). When the race started, Bev flew off at the first corner, Tony Brise blew an engine, Dave Morgan went wide and damaged his nose cone, while I hung in there and won the race. Fantastic! I gave Mr Nestlé Van a job-list of what I wanted done before the next race at Oulton Park, but when I got up there, the car was still in the transporter and what was more, it had never been out of the transporter; absolutely nothing had been done.

'Do we do this right?' I asked him. 'Because if you don't get this car right, I'm not going to race for you.' I wasn't asking him to spend a whole lot of money; it was mostly minor, mechanical things. But there are lots of fly-by-nights at that level of racing; they don't really have the cash or the guts to do a job properly. I knew we'd been lucky to win that race at Silverstone. I'd made a great impression in a car that was a shit-ache. If I went on driving that car, things could only get worse; people would forget Silverstone and my name would be mud. From which I concluded that I should get out while the going was good.

I went round to all the people who had good cars at Silverstone and I told them why I was withdrawing from the race: because my man had done nothing to the car, and I was in racing to get results and not just to ponce about. That was when I saw Harry Stiller again. He'd congratulated me at Silverstone, and now he said, what are you doing next Wednesday? He must have known the answer, which was that I was doing nothing, but it was nice of him to put it that way. Harry Stiller and George Robinson are the two people I owe my racing career to. All right, said Harry, come up to Silverstone and have a test in my car. He had a brand-new March 74 and he had good engines. I hesitated not.

When I got to Silverstone that Wednesday, Bev Bond had been complaining that Harry's car had terminal understeer. I had therefore asked Robin Herd to be there while we tested, and he and I spent most of a morning going through a set of front tyres trying to dial out the understeering.

A car, unless its steering, its tyres, its suspension and everything else is in perfect condition, is so sensitive in its responses to the wheel that 'understeering' and 'oversteering' are probably the two major complaints from drivers. The former means that when the driver uses his wheel, the car does not respond instantly, and it takes more effort on the wheel to get the car to turn properly; the latter means that the slightest tweak of the wheel does too much.

But by two in the afternoon I was going round a second quicker than the lap record, and by four I had taken a second-and-a-half off the record. Old Harry was over the moon about it and waving contracts all over the place. Bev Bond was to be chief mechanic, I was to drive for Harry the rest of the year and the bloke with his van and his unpaid bills was to be left to his own devices. And serve him right. I'd found not only a real man and a proper team, but a friend.

Every race that March did, we broke a record. We broke something like ten lap records that year. The only thing wrong with us was that, as the overworked Bev was doubling as chief mechanic and team manager, our reliability left something to be desired. A fact I ascertained by the way the gears came out in my hand for three races in a row. But while the car was going, it was the quickest thing on the circuit, bar none. We may not have won the Championship, but we'd impressed all the right people. Next year Formula 5000. Off to the show, look over the new Lolas, top of the world, everything's rosy. A.J. finally made it. Or has he?

As usual in sporting sagas, people like A.J. make it sound as though motor racing were all they did. They breakfast, lunch and dine on cars and engines. It isn't true. At that level of racing, there is never enough money to do that. Harry Stiller paid for A.J.'s car. He didn't pay for Alan's food or his house or for the girl he had since married. Real life goes on with its own kind of deadly persistence. We are now coming up to 1975; A.J. has been racing cars for five years; he has had three fairly successful seasons in Formula Three. This should be his year. In fact, Harry Stiller was to be A.J.'s turning point, but he didn't know that yet. His mind was on how to make a living.

I had a mate who had a boarding house in London, and when he explained to me how his system worked, it just seemed such a beautifully simple idea. What you had to do was borrow a friend's Rolls or some other posh car, front up to the biggest house you could see that was for sale or rent and then go up and ring the bell. The lady of the house or whoever would come out and you'd say (being as nicely-spoken as you could for an Aussie), 'Hello, how are you? I'm an Australian and my father owns one of those huge sheep-stations back home. I'd like to rent this house for a year.' The lady would look at you and say, 'How many are you?' And you'd answer, very correctly, 'There's only my wife and myself at present, but of course Father will be coming over with Mama later in the year during the sheep off-season' – or some tale like that. 'That's why we want such a big house.'

I learned early: dress well, speak well, drive a good car and nobody asks, 'Can you afford whatever it is you're trying to buy?'

What we'd do was rent a five- or six-bedroom house, then I'd go down to the Army and Navy and buy a batch of double-decker bunks, respray them chocolate brown, put two double-deckers and a little garbage can in each room and rent the rooms out, four people to a room at eleven quid a week each with breakfast. Bloody gold-mine. You do breakfast from 7 to 9, tidy up their rooms once a week and you're off and running. Bev and I would rent to Australians, New Zealanders, Americans and Canadians only: if they were local, why would they pay that price to share a bedroom with three others, unless they were deadbeats?

Our Aussies were all under thirty. What they wanted was a warm and comfortable base until they bought their caravans and took off for the magical mystery tour of Europe. Under normal circumstances, in Australia, they wouldn't be seen dead living as they did with us; but in London they were prepared for everything, England being an expedition for them. And sometimes you could flog them a caravan over the breakfast table.

With Harry Stiller's drive coming up and myself married and the money coming in, I thought I could relax over that Christmas. No, I got the annual telephone call. It was Harry Stiller, sounding very apologetic and at least honest: he'd lost all his sponsorship, he was sorry, but I'd better start looking right away for an alternative drive. Here we go again! I had an awful January and February; my professional life was going hot, cold, hot, cold every week.

Then Harry pulled this miracle out of his hat. One day he just called me out of the blue. 'Look,' he said, 'I'm as tired of pissing about as you are, so I've done a deal with Hesketh. You're going to race a Formula One Hesketh.' I couldn't believe it. A few months ago I was going to race a very good semi-works Formula 5000 car; for two months I'd been professionally unemployed and wondering if I would ever drive again, and now I'd got a drive in a bloody Formula One car. Miraculous!

Part 2

Formula One, But Not All is Roses

Alexander, Lord Hesketh, the scion of a grocery fortune and a member by his mother of the McEwen clan of writers and painters, is one of the outsize figures that give motor racing a certain piquancy. He was then in his mid-twenties, the owner of a great house at Towcester, a fat, ebullient, sporty sixties character, far from unshrewd and a splasher. It had entered his head — as it later entered the heads of Walter Wolf, an oil-exploration magnate, and David Thieme, whose authorized biography claims a start as an art-designer in love with violet and a finish as a millionaire petroleum broker — that motor racing was a fun scene. Consequently he was putting together a Formula One team from scratch: with nought but money and some pretty savvy associates.

His manager, 'Bubbles' Horsley, was a man of patchy but occasionally brilliant talent. His number one driver was James Hunt, 'Master James' as he was christened, because of his genteel upbringing and sometimes deliberate rudeness. Master James was the man who had escaped his minor public school in a big, rebellious way: bare feet, filthy T-shirts, exquisite girls and all; but as a driver, he was both very quick, very aggressive and, as drivers at the time said, bloody dangerous. No one had a more spectacular record of accidents than Master James; hence his sobriquet of Hunt the Shunt. Hesketh did not mature Hunt — that was to come later with Teddy Mayer and the McLaren team — but it did give him his opportunity to do his stuff. That launched James, and Hesketh, by giving A.J. his big chance, effectively created the breakthrough in his career.

The Hesketh milieu was the total antithesis of A.J.'s lifestyle, as Alexander was everything that A.J. wasn't. And that first year chez Hesketh was Alexander's ragtime fling. Champagne and pheasants in hired marquees with Lady Hesketh, Alexander's

*mother, complete with black eye-patch, presiding in a state of
distraction; helicopters that flew ice and birds and more cham-
pers in and out of circuits; Master James among the Beautiful
People with the exquisite Susie, who dreamed of her piano-play-
ing childhood in Rhodesia and was about to leap away into
Richard Burton Land. It was a year of parties and night life,
some results, an ever-improving but never reliable car, which
couldn't last forever. Its very real sense of style is marked by a
scene probably apocryphal, but part of the legend, in the Brazilian rococo surroundings of the Copacabana Palace Hotel. Alexander was being turned away from the lift: ladies were not
allowed upstairs and Alexander had on his arm one of those
extremely black waifs that abound on Copacabana Beach. So the
tale goes, Alexander, all pink cheeks and fair hair, turned ma-
jestically on the lift attendant and said, 'This lady is my* sister!'

*In A.J.'s account of that brief brush with Society, there is a
strong residue of culture-shock: the transition from the Nestlé
chocolate van to the immaculate Hesketh garage at Towcester,
from Formula Three to Formula One, from boarding house to
mansion. And there is also the sweet whiff of chance, of Lady
Fortune suddenly smiling.*

When I drove up to the Hesketh headquarters and went up this
huge driveway and into the workshop, it was like going into
another world. Everything was in its place; the factory was
immaculate like a scrubbed surgery and when I was being fitted
into the car, if I wanted a quarter-inch off here or the steering
wheel lifted a bit, it was all, 'Yes, Mr Jones, no problem.' It was
another world from the grotty garages I had worked in. My car
was up on blocks, all the tools and the floor were spotless, they
even had a little box for me to stand on to climb into the car.
The mantle of the superstar was falling on me, with everyone
very attentive and highly professional. It's all very well for
people outside to look down on Alexander Hesketh and call him
a buffoon who just stumbled into motor racing; from the inside,
when it came down to the nitty-gritty of the business, they were
very, very professional. Bubbles Horsley was capable of getting
the very best out of Hunt, and in that respect it was a very good
team.

My first race for Hesketh was a non-championship event, the Daily Express race at Silverstone, and I finished seventh. That being my first-ever race in a Formula One car, everyone was very pleased, myself included. The whole scene was an eye-opener. I had no idea whether all Formula One teams were like Alexander's or whether I'd landed up in some extraordinarily exotic outfit. It's not in my nature to be thrown by externals: I didn't bother with the social scene; I just did my job.

I didn't actually penetrate the great house until 1979, when Bev and I stayed there during the British Grand Prix. We arrived at about eight o'clock, parked the car and went in to see where everyone was. They were all sitting at this fifty-foot long dining table with servants lurking about and Alexander ebullient as ever. I sat down and, after about twenty minutes of chat, I said I'd better go out to the car and bring in my gear. When I got out there, the car had been stripped. I thought someone had stolen all my stuff. But when we were shown to our room, there it was, all unpacked and laid out on the bed, the toilet stuff in the bathroom.

I was on pole that weekend and every evening we dressed for dinner: and eight or ten miles down the road were the fumes and the screaming noise. It was a little weird. It would have been a perfect weekend if I'd won the race: I had pole, I led the race but had to retire. But I always got on well with Alexander. He treated me fairly and everyone made me feel very welcome. They didn't look on me as some sort of hired hand or a paid drive – get out of the way, son, you're just here to supplement our racing budget. There was none of that.

A.J.'s first Formula One Grand Prix was at Barcelona in 1975. Practice in Formula One is split over two days, with two untimed and two timed practices, the latter deciding the starting positions on the grid. The Formula One paddock was located in what was once a Roman-type circus on top of the park of Montjuic. The motor-homes were spacious and scattered: A.J. wandered about, taking in the complex mechanisms that make Formula One tick at such a different pace from the rest of motor-sport. He was a new boy and treated as such: with curiosity by those who had manners and superciliousness by those who didn't.

When I came up into Formula One, the big names were people like Emerson Fittipaldi, Ronnie Peterson, Niki Lauda and James Hunt: particularly James, who seemed to like living his life bathed in brilliant publicity. It was something I had to get used to having around me, though I was just a beginner and nobody paid all that much attention to me. It was still an odd sensation to see my name and picture in the papers: even when I couldn't understand what they were saying about me.

You get no help from other drivers when you start out in Formula One. The drivers who are part of the scene and have been for some time come in two kinds: the ones who make you feel welcome, and the ones who snub you. I was a new boy, and tradition dictates that you snub new boys. It was like going to a new school; you have to force your way in.

In Spain some drivers came up and said hello and made me feel welcome; others walked right past me as though I weren't there. Emerson was always polite; Carlos Reutemann was one of the friendly ones; Jochen Mass was one of the nicest – but then he's just a supremely nice man. Too nice to be a racing driver, some say, though that's not my opinion; Jochen driving, as far as I can see, just as hard as the rest of us, but never having a first-class team at the right time.

A number of drivers were just neutral: they did their own thing and left me alone to get on with mine. Tom Pryce was nice, but very shy. As for the ones who snubbed me in 1975: they were the ones who were going out of their way to be nice in 1978 and 1979 when I started winning. And when it came to the end of 1979 and I had to help pick my Number Two driver for 1980, they were more than just ordinarily friendly!

I can understand why they don't help you out. I would not myself presume to go up to a new driver and give him advice. He might be a better driver than I am. It would be different if he were a younger team-mate: Clay Regazzoni and Carlos Reutemann were both helpful to me and I to them. We'd swop information. We were driving very similar cars; we could legitimately help each other. But basically I'm very reluctant to tell anyone anything. You never know: the man you help could be your enemy tomorrow. I have my own career to think about. Why should I help some newcomer to blow me off?

49

Barcelona, 1975 – First Time Out

Barcelona 1975 was a race marred by the inadequate safety of the beautiful circuit that meanders up and down and around through the Montjuic park. The protest, which soon turned into a strike by the drivers, was led by Emerson Fittipaldi, always a leader – joined now by the 1979 World Champion, Jody Scheckter – in the cause of safety. Closely involved was the enigmatic and very intelligent Bernard Ecclestone, the master-mind of Formula One and the man who promoted the sport from amateurism to the status of an international event.

The protest provided a glimpse of the callousness which marks many of the constructors' attitudes towards driver safety. 'Drivers,' a number of them said bellicosely, not for the first or last time, 'are paid to race; let them get on with it!' And Bernard Ecclestone hopped like a bird from motor-home to motor-home and round the track trying to resolve a strike that was, then wasn't, then was and finally wasn't.

When the race finally started, there was no indication of the real magnitude of the risks involved in the sport. Less than an hour later, there was a much clearer vision of those dangers. Not far from the paddock a wing flew off Rolf Stommelen's car, and car and Stommelen catapulted over the freshly installed armco to kill five spectators.

I can hardly remember where I was in the race. I know I didn't finish. But I remember the drama clearly: all of us sitting in the Grand Prix Drivers' Association trailer arguing about safety. What had I got myself into? Politics? A debating club? It's extraordinary the heat that can be raised at those meetings. There are always people at both extremes, and only a few in the middle. If anything, I sympathized with the get-on-with-the-race group. I knew I wasn't in Barcelona to sit in a motor-home and argue about armco and fencing. Now I might be a bit more conscious of that, but back then I had only my own little world to think about.

My second grand prix for Hesketh was at Monaco. There were only eighteen starters allowed and I only just scraped in, last qualified. Graham Hill didn't qualify and some other hot-shots didn't either. With about ten minutes to go in the last practice session, I seemed to be definitely out of the race. All I remember now of the heat of the moment is that I put on a set of new tyres and went out on the track as hard as I knew how; and when the flag showed practice was over, I remember sitting in the pits waiting for the PA system to tell me if I'd made it. They read it out, starting painfully at the front and after seventeen other names, I finally heard mine! The celebrations in the Hesketh pits were as if just qualifying were winning a grand prix. I was lying tenth in that race when a wheel came off.

After Monaco, it was Zolder in Belgium, where I managed to qualify on the same row as James. I was the new-found hero and Alexander at that stage was frothing around saying he would run two cars the next year for James and myself. The days were still whacky. We were like a menagerie of kids out from school. A bloke called Tom Parks who owned a restaurant was cooking up bacon and eggs for the mechanics; at the other end of the social scale Alexander was reclining in the motor-home strapped into all these tubes and an oxygen mask trying to come back to life after a monumental hangover.

Hesketh breathed life into A.J.'s career but, reading between the lines, it has to be said that it lacked the higher kind of seriousness and single-mindedness that A.J. wanted. And there weren't all that many places for an Australian driver to go. Jack Brabham had built his own team: he was constructor and driver, an example that Bruce McLaren sought to emulate. On the whole, Formula One racing is as much bedevilled by national rivalries as any other international sport. For the first ten years of the modern Formula One championship, the sport was almost totally dominated by the Italians; since the early sixties it has been largely a British-dominated sport, with the French lately making a strong bid to enter the top ranks.

To their everlasting credit, the British are prepared to help anyone who deserves it, regardless of nationality, and I don't owe any part of my racing career to Australians. They didn't back me when I started and they only paid attention to me when I won the Championship. But two Englishmen, George Robinson and Harry Stiller, put it on the line for me when it counted. You wouldn't find a French team or sponsor doing for a young foreign driver what those two did for me; and if the Italians did anything it would be strictly out of self-interest. The help George Robinson gave me was unbeatable: he had faith in my ability, he thought I would make it and he backed his judgment in ways that really told in my career.

Harry Stiller is a wheeler-dealer from Bournemouth, a shareholder in the Rob Walker group and also involved in a sort of pub-fun affair down his way. Once I'd driven in Formula Atlantic for Harry, he was determined to get me into Formula One, whatever the obstacles. He put a fair amount of his own bread on the line and had to talk to a lot of people before he got me that drive with Hesketh. I wouldn't be where I am without him.

It's funny how things work out. Around the middle of 1975, Harry decided he wanted to go and live in America; I think the taxes in England were getting to him, as they get to all of us. He told me not to worry, he would fix an American Formula 5000 for me. But whereas a few months before I'd been dying to drive anything at all, now I had four grands prix under my belt and I'd been bitten by the bug. I thought I could make it in Formula One. In fact I thought I could be World Champion, and I didn't welcome the thought of quitting Formula One to go race in the unknown in the States.

But fate always seems to play a part. So much of this game is just luck. First, there was Rolf Stommelen having his big accident in Barcelona; that put Rolf out of commission for a fair bit of the season. Then there was Graham Hill, who ran the Embassy-Hill team for which Stommelen had driven, hearing on the grapevine that old Harry was taking off to the States and that I might be without a drive. He asked me if I would take Rolf's place until he recovered. Needless to say I accepted.

I had another four grands prix for Graham Hill then, but it wasn't the happiest period of my life. The two most difficult people I've ever driven for were two ex-champions, Graham Hill and John Surtees. Socially, butter wouldn't melt in Graham's mouth; he could charm snakes out of the trees. He was a superb diplomat and I learned a lot from him. I've seen him turn from a heated debriefing argument into a smiling jovial snake-oil salesman: all it required was that someone from outside should walk in the door. The moment that someone left, his smile would vanish and it would be back to business. A great show-man, a great ambassador, but a wretched man to work for. Having been a world champion, he knew better than any driver how to set up a car. He wouldn't listen to advice. He was stubborn and inflexible. As a result, every car I drove for Graham was different; no two were ever alike.

A sensitive subject, the preparation, or setting-up of a car. Normally, it is a strictly co-operative effort between the team engineer and the driver, with occasional wisdom from the constructor – especially when, as with Colin Chapman, for instance, the constructor is himself an engineer. This preparation is an arcane art, and revolves around the literally hundreds of minor adjustments to the basic car that will make it handle better on a given day on a given track: suspensions, brakes, tyre compounds and the like. Graham Hill was no engineer but, having been a driver, thought he was one. A smart engineer listens to his driver. His driver is the man who literally 'feels' the car, who knows its every sound and response. Hence A.J.'s bitterness.

Graham's car understeered like a pig. It was almost impossible to handle, and when Stommelen did come back to the team, he had exactly the same trouble with the car and with Graham that I did; it ended in a flaming row and Rolf quit. A decision I can well understand. In spite of that car, I did manage to score more points for the Hill team than anyone had before, or since, and Graham asked me to come back and test their new car at Ricard. Only a few weeks after that, Tony Brise and Graham were down at Ricard testing and were killed when Graham crashed his plane on the way back to England. It could easily have been me.

1975 was coming to a close and, once again, I had nothing at all lined up for 1976. I had the odd telephone call, I had promises, I had hints, but nothing solid. I had a midnight call from Louis Stanley, a real waffler if ever there was one. There are some cars you don't want to drive and some people you don't want to drive for. Lou Stanley was one of the latter kind, and his car came to be known as the Stanley Steamer because on the track it behaved just like an old-fashioned tea-kettle. He gave me the business as he always did, about how wonderful his car was, how wonderful he was, how wonderful his organization was. I just didn't believe him; not about himself, not about his car.

The next to call was John Surtees. He said, a bit loftily I thought, that he was trying out a few new boys and would I care to come down and test his car. I thought it strange that after seven or eight grands prix he still didn't know what I was like, and if he didn't know by then, how would he ever learn? But beggars can't be choosers. I went down, put in some pretty competitive times and John said I had the drive for 1976.

It should be made plain at this point that Formula One does not consist exclusively of glamorous, successful teams like Lotus or Ferrari. Alongside the colossi are the midgets. The sport is full of survivors. Some of them never have and never will see a world championship, though every last one of them would deny that their aim was to achieve anything else but. And many of them which have produced world champions in the past survive almost wholly on the vestiges of that past glory, for sponsors will apparently always believe that those who once had the magic will have it again: for instance Teddy Mayer and the McLaren team, who have been in a fallow period since James Hunt, or Ken Tyrrell, whose drought has been even longer and deeper.

And there is ample evidence that the failures of today may be the successes of tomorrow. That is what keeps hope alive. Particularly when constructors consider the case of A.J.'s own Frank Williams. No one's memory is so short that he cannot remember the days when Frank was publicly considered to be a rank outsider – a nice, hard-working little man who would never get anywhere. With Frank, the missing ingredient proved to be money. Once he got Arab sponsorship, Frank's cars swept the board: the talent was latent.

But the choices for a driver of talent, at least until he has truly proved himself, are limited. Every once in a while a new private team, like Walter Wolf, will come along, take a Jody Scheckter and a lot of money, and create a sort of overnight miracle. Other private sponsors, like David Thieme, will back Lotus with mil-

lions at a time when the team itself and its cars are no longer
competitive.

Bottom and middle-of-the-field drivers, such as A.J. was in
1975 and 1976, are stuck in a terrible bind. In the eyes of the top
teams – meaning those who are competitive in any given year –
they have not done enough to rate a place in their cars. Yet in
their own eyes, those drivers have done more than enough to
deserve something better than a no-hope team. Faced with this
unpalatable choice, and granted the axiom that it is always better
to race than not to race, a driver's only hope is to show how well
he can do in spite of his inadequate team and car.

As is so often the case at the beginning of a driving career in
Formula One, getting a drive at all is hard enough, and almost
always complicated by the involved deals that are required to
make that bit of magic possible. In the case of John Surtees, or
Don Nichols of Shadow a year later (both of whom were doing
no better than surviving as small fry among the bigger and
better constructors) the deal involved a deep question of money.
Don Nichols didn't have enough; John Surtees had just enough,
but it came from an American driver called Brett Lunger. Lunger had all sorts of money behind him, but, in my opinion,
nothing very spectacular or ferocious in terms of driving skills.
Brett was to get his car first, since he was paying for the team,
and I would get mine as soon as it was built.

It wasn't a happy season, though it could have been, because
the TS9 was a pretty good little car to drive. We missed the two
South American races at the beginning of the season, and when
I hauled my body down to South Africa to get an idea of how
the team was working, I got all of three laps at Kyalami and
that was it; a bloody waste of time. My first race for Surtees
was at the Race of Champions at Brands Hatch. I arrived on
the track and walked around everywhere looking for our transporter; it hadn't even arrived. When it did arrive, just before
the practice session, there was the panic and frenzy I came to
associate with John's running of the team.

I had to take the car out literally untried. It was spanking
new, but luckily, because it was a wet, greasy sort of day,
preparing the chassis didn't count for much; it was a matter of

having some track knowledge and just having a go. I qualified about sixth quickest and led James Hunt for most of the race, with the car getting better and better as the track dried out. James finally overtook me, but I finished second and everyone was running around saying our car was obviously going to be *the* car for that season. Except that we went to Long Beach and only just scraped onto the grid.

I had a very fraught time driving for Big John. He was like Graham Hill in that he thought he knew everything there was to know about racing; he presumed that because I was relatively new to the Championship, I knew nothing. Every time I changed gears in that car I scraped the skin off my knuckles. I asked John to put a bubble on the side of the cockpit. He wouldn't do it: he thought it would look funny if there wasn't a bubble on the other side of the cockpit. It just wouldn't look symmetrical. Damn symmetry, I thought; I'd rather be able to change my gears and not come away bleeding. To my mind if a driver wants a bubble or a bloody purple pole between his legs, he should get it. One of the reasons Frank Williams is so good is that if he thinks anything will make you happier or quicker, you'll get it. He trusts his drivers.

If all this argument over a bubble seems ridiculous, it should be remembered that team managers and designers are understandably wary of the demands drivers make on them. A considerable number of drivers are readily inclined to blame their own failures on the car. Designers do the same: blame drivers for weaknesses in their cars. This is more than failure of communication. Egos are involved, which designers have no less than drivers. Some designers, though not the best, think of drivers as replaceable light bulbs to be screwed in to the car they provide which, in their minds, does all the work. Drivers at least know the value of the better designers. But it is frustrating for a designer who thinks, always, that he has produced the perfect racing vehicle, to realize that he cannot climb into the cockpit himself and prove his point.

At the top of the profession, obviously, the relationship between designer, engineer, team-manager and driver is symbiotic. At the middle and bottom, running warfare is a more natural state.

Like Graham, John was simply reluctant to get out of the cock-pit. It is a phenomenon among retired racing drivers. Though the cars and the conditions change from season to season, former drivers always think they know best. If they turn constructors, like Graham and John, their driver is just a surrogate for them-selves: they live in the motor racing world through their driver, they identify with him, they experience through him. But they are not in the car.

John would take our car down to Goodwood and test it without any bloody wings. All right, except for the fact that if you take the wings off, you've got to change the spring rates to compen-sate for the extra down-force. But John would go down and take the car around in a leisurely 1.12 and pronounce it beautiful; I'd go down there and take it around in 1.9 and it would be a shambles. Any time you take a car out as though you were taking the kids out for a drive, it's likely to feel marvellously good; it's only when you put the real stresses on that the car begins to hurt.

It took us four months to develop a nose on the car that would generate more downforce. *(Downforce is what keeps the car on the track at high speeds and on curves; without the design fea-tures that produce downforce, one part or another of the car will have a tendency to lift off the surface. The alternatives when it does lift are either to slow down or to fly.)* It was always the same story: John would fiddle with the car, I'd go out and practise and come back to tell John what the car needed, he'd fiddle some more, I'd practise some more, and, if I was lucky, it was at about the end of the second practice that I'd get the car back to the shape it was the last time we went racing.

We always had to go through the rigmarole of John insisting on his opinions; sometimes it was as though we were re-invent-ing the wheel. It was a shame, because it was a sound little car, the right shape and very quick in a straight line. If Patrick Head, our designer at Williams, had got his hands on that car, it would have been a world championship car. It had the right stuff.

It took me until the German Grand Prix at the Nürburgring to get the bubble on my cockpit. I was having a nice dice with Vittorio Brambilla in a March and found I was backing up all the dog rings in the gear box because I just couldn't get it into gear. Fate would have it that Vittorio, who had been through two chassis that weekend, should be close enough to take me off during the race, just as we were going down into the Adenau Bridge. We touched and I spun down the hill, spun again on the bridge and wound up with the nose of the car in the gutter. I got going again, running about ninth or tenth and literally had to do the last two laps without being able to get into third or fourth gears. After the race, I screamed and yelled at John and showed him my hand which was scraped raw through my gloves, and by the next race I had my bubble.

Was it all necessary? I found it unprofessional. His ego got in the way of the team. That convinced me that having come to the end of 1976 and having raced for Hesketh and Graham Hill and John Surtees, I was actually no longer interested in another Formula One drive unless I could get myself into a properly professional team. I felt I couldn't keep on running around in circles any more, and if Surtees wouldn't release me from my contract, I'd go over to the United States and do a season of USAC racing.

This alternative, rich pickings and all, is always available to Formula One drivers. That they don't flock there in quantity is due to a number of factors: it is provincial racing in provincial places without any of the accoutrements or perks of Formula One; and it is oval racing, round and round a circuit, which most Formula One drivers consider slightly infra dig. USAC racing may be as professional and as competitive, but it is also both tamer and wilder, as A.J. was to find out.

Racing in America under American regulations is a different world, a highly protected world. Over there, if an aeroplane flies under the sun, they cancel practice because there's a shadow on the track. It's a joke. I got there a week too early to do testing: I've never spent so much time in overalls or done so little work in my life. I was there for three or four days and never so much as turned a wheel because it was too windy.

The day for qualifying finally came up and I got in about twenty minutes of practice with everyone out on the circuit.

There were A. J. Foyt and all those guys doing 200-odd miles an hour and I was out in a McLaren which, it transpired, was a pig; I couldn't get the hang of the thing and I was just a mobile chicane. In everybody's interest, I withdrew from the race. It was not an easy decision. Teddy Yip had hired the car, put his Chinese hieroglyphics all over it and flown from Australia just to be there, and there was his driver saying he's not going to drive. Everyone tried to talk me out of my decision; they said I'd get the hang of it during the race.

That's just not the way I care to race. If there was some idiot on the track in Formula One, potentially dangerous and getting in my way, I'd want him off the track. Oval racing was just not for me. It's primitive. They don't practise, they don't prepare their cars or themselves, they just hop in and go out. It's also bloody dangerous. An accident affects everyone. I could be well back in the field when someone up front loses it; there's every chance he's going to get me. What happens is: his car goes up and hits the wall, it disintegrates and you've got wheels, monocoques and wings spraying down on you. Or he bounces off the wall, hits somebody else and three or four of you go the same way. If I have one of the big ones, I'd like to think I caused it, rather than just being a victim.

'Losing it' is a key term in the racing lexicon. Such are the stresses, the speeds, the intensity and rapidity of the decisions that have to be taken, that when something goes wrong, it really is a 'loss' rather than an 'error'. The human animal who sits in the machine cannot, at all times, control every variable at his command, and the variables extend well beyond his own performance and the reliability of his car, to the track, other drivers, other cars and a multitude of other factors. The forces are such, and the speed, that each and every manoeuvre, every curve, every overtaking, is a point of maximum risk. If everything is not in perfect order, the driver is not in much of a position to avert catastrophe. When something goes terribly wrong, he may minimize its effects, he may avert the worst, but he knows for certain that he's going to lose it. Centimetres and microseconds are the measure of the gap between safety and shunt.

Like much of the jargon of the sport, 'losing it' conceals more

than it reveals, particularly when it comes to assigning the blame
for any mishap. There is almost no way to record the failure. Or
whose failure it was. Formula One cars carry no little black boxes
to record the critical moments before a crash. Often enough, when
the driver survives, which is in the vast majority of cases – and
always surprisingly, when you survey the wreckage of the car –
he cannot explain what happened. He 'lost it'; just as not to
survive is referred to as so-and-so 'bought it'.

In 1979 I actually raced again in America. It was a so-called
'International Race of Champions' in which all the drivers are
kitted out with supposedly identical Chevrolet Camaros. After
my experience in the McLaren in 1976, I thought those big old
Chevvys, with the big roll-cages across them, were safe enough.

The scene was pleasant. The American drivers were friendly.
One of the NASCAR blokes showed me some of the tricks of
the trade, such as how they can position their car behind you in
such a way as to make you oversteer, or induce terminal understeer. Very keen to help, they were; or maybe they were just
keen that I should know what I was doing.

I was out testing, having done the second quickest time on
the oval. Peter Gregg, who was known as Peter Perfect, decided
he'd join in the fun. There were two cars behind me, the second
car being Peter's. Suddenly Peter pulled out from behind the
car that was on my tail and drafted *(to 'draft' someone is to use*
the slipstream in the wake of their car to gain additional speed
for overtaking: the vacuum in the wake of a racing car will
actually pull a following car forward) past both of us as we went
into Turn Three. Which was where Peter lost it. He went broad-
side right along the middle of the track. The driver behind me
chose to go below Peter; I tried to get above him, between Peter
and the wall. If you lose it in oval racing, what you're meant to
do is turn in to the slide and spin your car into the infield, but
Peter, being a road-racer like myself, did what I would have
done in the same conditions to correct the slide: he corrected it
and shot straight up into the wall.

I was doing about 170 m.p.h. when I T-boned him. I went
from his car into the wall and from the wall back into him,
completely demolishing the Camaro. At first I thought I'd really

hurt myself badly: I hit him so hard, I lost all the fluid out of my body. My mouth just flew open, I felt all this fluid all over my body and I thought I'd haemorrhaged.

I think in a big one like that, a driver always thinks the worst. I'd hit him at 170 m.p.h., gone straight into the concrete wall and pushed the engine right up through the body of the car so that the Camaro was about four feet shorter. I was completely winded; I couldn't breathe. Luckily, all I had was a very bad case of bruising, but for a few seconds I had a clear picture of myself being dragged out of the car and raced to hospital.

When I hit him, it was as though I'd come right out of my seat and been suspended against my safety belts; it was as though someone had taken a tar brush and painted marks on my body where the seat belts had been. The next day I felt as though I'd had third-degree sunburn; I could barely move. But I thought, hold on here, if this happened in a big safe old Chevvy Camaro, think what that shunt would have been like in a little fragile USAC car like I'd tried in 1976. It didn't take much to convince me, after that, that there was no way in the world I would go USAC racing again. Ever.

Drivers have a sort of elementary prudence. They minimize risk wherever possible and always seek the maximum protection: Nomex overalls, visors, asbestos gloves and face-masks. But such prudential thought is in direct contrast to the risks they have no choice but to take. It is just those risks they are paid to run. Formula One cars are phenomenally safe, at least compared with the cars that you and I drive. But not all are equally safe, and none is safe at all times. Some designers build stronger – hence safer – cars than others; some will sacrifice safety for speed.

Accidents are a subject on which most drivers are both reticent and evasive. On the average, a driver will have a major accident once every eleven grands prix and a relatively serious injury every other major shunt. But it is not merely that they are reticent; their offtakes in fact are paradoxical. Most look on the fact of accident and injury with a cold eye. But that is in the abstract. In most situations, they reject the evidence of their own minds. Accidents happen to others: that is the guiding principle of the driver, and in that convenient evasion, the thought of accidents

61

would be inadmissible. What is a driver thinking about as he reaches the point of no return?

Even when a shunt seems inevitable, you fight it right up to the end: until it really *is*. When that moment comes, everything is happening so quickly that a driver doesn't really have much time to do anything, nor even think very much. I go into a state that is not really a daze so much as an acceptance of the inevitable. My thought is: 'It's going to happen; I've got to make sure I get out of this alive.'

At the time of impact, everything is happening so quickly that I am simultaneously aware of its happening and of its inevitability. The G-forces throw a driver's hands all over the place. It's not as though he could react calmly and throw the car into neutral or shut off the master switch: not while he's banging into the wall. At that stage he is just being knocked about. He is a dead weight, a human dummy. His next positive reaction is when he finally comes to rest. His first thought is probably to check his body out in all its particulars: is he all there? is anything radically wrong? Almost simultaneously he will turn off the master switch – because fire is what every driver dreads most – and the next thing he'll do, if he's not winded or unconscious or unable, is jump out of the car and get away from it as quickly as possible. The worst things occur when you stay in too long; and that only happens when you can't get out.

In that shunt with Peter, I was badly winded, I was confused, I didn't know what this liquid was; obviously the straps had pulled with such violence against my belly that they forced out everything I'd drunk that morning. I was winded and dazed to the point where I couldn't move. At the same time I could see the car was steaming and I was thinking, 'Let's hope this bleeder doesn't catch fire, because if it does, I don't know how quickly I can move. And as I thought that, I was also hoping and praying the marshalls would get to me quickly and move me out.

There are really three stages. In the first, you're still fighting for control, still trying to prevent the accident, even when you know your chances are minimal. That stage continues until you know it is going to happen and there's nothing at all you can do about it. At the impact, you don't think at all. Your mind is a blank. From that point until you come to a standstill is stage two: it happens so quickly and so violently there is time neither to think nor to do, you're in the lap of the gods. There are huge, loud noises, there are wrenches and twists, lurches, bangs, forces twisting you every which way: it's like being set upon by a gang of thugs in an alley. When you come to a stop finally, which is the third stage, you realize that you're still alive and functioning – and if you're not, you don't really know it – and then your mind can start working again on what to do next.

Consider the case of Irish driver John Watson after his head-on collision with the tyres and fencing at Ricard in 1980. John said that when he knew he was going to hit that wall head on, it was as though there had been a break in his computer system. His programme had instructed him in all the things he had to do to avoid or minimize the accident, but when the defence system failed, it was a curiously lonely feeling, as though he'd been abandoned by his thinking machine and found himself mentally naked at the moment of impact. The prospect of hitting that wall head-on had stolen his mind and suddenly the gap between the capacity of his computer, which you could also call his driving experience, his know-how, and the situation that computer was facing, had become intolerably large.

I don't think there's a gap between conscious and subconscious thought during a shunt. It's largely a question of whether I have time to do any thinking of any kind at all, conscious or subconscious. In a way, even one's reflexes dry up. Once you accept that there's nothing your mind can do, that there are no longer any effective orders it can give, you ride it out.

Perhaps it's not that you lack the time to think. It may be that you don't *want* to think. Perhaps what a driver feels is resignation, a refusal to acknowledge what is happening to him, or even outrage that it *is*. I do not sit there helplessly and think about anything outside the car. I'm not looking at my past life or thinking of my boy or the bills I've forgotten to pay. I know something is happening, but I don't actually think about any-thing. The body isn't paralyzed; it isn't that you can't move or twitch. It's a form of knowing that nothing your body can do will help.

Meanwhile, however, you observe everything that is going on. Very acutely and almost abstractly. It is happening, and it is happening to you. When I T-boned Peter Gregg, I knew I was going to a split second before I actually did. I kept my eyes wide open and, after I hit him, I saw very clearly that my car was bouncing off him and heading straight for the wall. You don't think: you register a fact. The fact is in the form of a thought: 'Oh Christ! I'm going to have a big one, I'm going to hit the bloody wall!' I hit the wall and registered coming away from the wall and sliding down the embankment. At that point I knew that, as far as crunching into things went, the accident was finished. I'd been through the worst.

I was lucky that it happened during a practice session and that there were only three cars on the track. During a race, I would have sat there just as helplessly, but I would have registered another fact: that I was going to be hit; someone was going to whack into me.

A mixture, then, of phlegm, experience and intelligence. A driver goes through a sufficient number of shunts in his career to hone his reactions down to the point where each emergency results in its own drill, a sequence of moves designed to reduce the chances of the worst happening. Some of these moves are reflex actions, some are instinct and experience, others are the product of pure chance.

For us, a drive in a Formula One car at the speeds a professional driver takes for granted, and in the competitive environment on which he thrives, would be a constant emergency. Our systems would be constantly overloaded. It is not so different even for the professional driver. A rough calculation suggests some sixty manoeuvres on an average lap. At an average of some seventy laps per race, that makes over 4000 manoeuvres inside two hours. Each manoeuvre probably requires at least four or five mental operations and another four or five physical manipulations – perhaps 40,000 in the average race. The wonder is that racing drivers are by and large so successful in avoiding mistakes.

What you do when you face a potential accident depends very much on its nature. I had a big one at Donington in 1980. I was testing some new radial tyres and the tread flew off one; one moment I was barrelling down the straight as fast as I could go, the next the car was turned left into the armco and I went bouncing off it all the way down the straight. I was as if glued to the armco, and I couldn't get the car to steer at all; it kept pulling into the wall. I knew the car was badly damaged, but I concentrated on riding it out, taking my hands off the wheel so that if it wrenched very quickly, it wouldn't break my fingers.

It seemed a huge distance down the straight when the tread flew off, but by the time I'd decided what I would try to do, there wasn't any straight left. I had no brakes because my left wheel was down in front and my right wheel up in back. I was still going fast and coming up to the escape road. Great, I thought, I'll just slide up the escape road and come to a stop. Unfortunately, there was also a little ditch and then a succession of eight-foot tall concrete posts. It hit me that when I came to the end of the armco, I was going to turn left and start mowing down the concrete posts.

I put my head down and mowed into the first three or four and the fifth one actually flipped up; it flicked the top of my dashboard and flew straight over my head. From the dashboard down on my car it's all skin and no open space, but for sure, if I hadn't ducked, that cement post would have taken my head off. When I got out of the car, the whole of its left side was ripped right off and the front had a huge dent where the post had end-over-ended and gone right over my cockpit. I was just lucky that day. And sometimes a simple reflex will save your life. I didn't think, 'Here's that post coming, now I'd better duck'; I just ducked.

When a shunt like that happens, the driver quickly unstraps himself and jumps out of the cockpit. He will take a brief look back at the car, as though verifying that it and he are still there, and then start the long walk back to the pits. In a half-sentence or two, he will explain what happened: the steering locked, I lost it on the curve, the brakes gave out, my throttle stuck open. For him, that takes care of the matter, and the rest is history. But the smart ones, the older ones, the more experienced ones, know how finely balanced is the line between good and ill-fortune. That was a close one, they will say with a shake of the head. It is part of the tradition, as when any of us is conscious of a lucky escape. But they do what most of us would not do: they go right out again. And know the next close escape cannot be far off. Will they be lucky the next time?

To me, the worst shunts of all are when a throttle gets stuck open. Because when that happens, the shunt is almost bound to be a big one. You know what you have to do: you've got to declutch and blow your engine up – anything to get some of the speed off. If you can de-clutch, that stops your back wheels spinning. And if you've got time to do that, maybe you have time to flick the kill switch, too. But jamming on the brakes, which is what most of us would do instinctively, is of no use at all. The moment you brake, you lose your steering, and then you inevitably go head first into whatever you're trying to steer away from.

It happened to me at Zandvoort in 1980. I was on a really quick lap and had just come out of the right-hander before the Hanserug, which I usually go into a little bit sideways, keeping my foot deep into it, braking at the last possible moment and then steering left to go up the hill. The trouble with corners like that, in which a driver will commit himself very deep, is that if anything goes wrong there is no time or space for him to either get around the corner or do anything to avoid an accident. That day, it was getting towards the close of practice and I went in very deep indeed. When I took my foot off the accelerator, that made no difference at all. The throttle was jammed wide open. What was the point of thinking about avoidance? I was in the fence before I could even consider evasive action. I gave that fence a proper whack.

But the strange thing is, the moment the car came to a rest, I didn't think what a lucky escape I'd had; I just thought, here it was, the last few minutes of practice and I'd messed up a good lap! My instinct was to jump out of the car and run back to the pits so I could go out in my spare.

Later, you might sit down and think about it. Then you say

to yourself, what the hell am I doing running back to my car when I should be running away from it! But I get so worked up and so obsessively concerned with a result, with being well up on the grid, that I'll brush by people and ignore the danger and do absolutely anything to get that result. It's a form of blindness, and as long as a driver can keep his mind working that way, with only his place on the grid or in the race counting, he's all right. It's when he starts to sit down afterwards and think, 'Christ! I might have been killed!' that he ought to start thinking about giving the game up.

The worst accident I ever had was not on a race-track. My friend Brian Maguire had bought a Ford Thunderbird and we were going to a party in Earls Court. The T-Bird is just about as poor-handling a car as you can buy, so it's undeniable that Brian should not have tried to out-corner a Lotus Elan. But he did and we just went straight into a brick wall, and from the brick wall, just as straight, into a tree. I took the door handle off with my ribs and went through the windscreen, busting my nose and shoulder.

All right, that time I knew I was seriously hurt. And if you've actually injured yourself, in a way that's easier. You know there's nothing you can do for yourself any more; you're totally in the hands of other people. I just lay back and let them get on with it. I was in a sort of day-dreamy daze. They put needles in you, cut you out of the metal, twist your body free from the wreckage. You just go along with whatever they're doing. You're a good boy, because it's their business to look after you now.

A.J. talks now about accidents and techniques and what the driver does with the assurance and loftiness that come from someone who has lived through the bad days and come into his own. The driver who is back among the also-rans has a different cast of mind. Often he does not see any exit at all from his particular blind alleys.

When I raced for Graham Hill or John Surtees, I felt I was just doing a job. I was glad when I'd finished my daily chores, whether it was practising, testing or racing. When I got a drive with Shadow in 1977, that was the beginning of a turning point for me. They were quite good to drive for. Don Nichols, who owned the team, may have been an odd, shadowy figure; a strange, lanky, bearded American who'd spent all those years in the Far East doing none of us knew what. But Alan Rees, the team manager, was one of the best in the business and, as a team, Shadow were very professional.

Having a good team-manager can change your whole outlook on racing. He breaks down the isolation you feel out there, alone in your car; he makes you feel that you belong to something besides yourself. Every good team-manager is a man who reads into a driver's mind with sympathy. He understands his driver's needs, he senses dissatisfactions, he is aware of the whole man, not just the employee who sits in the car and drives it. He is also as fiercely competitive as the man he is managing. If he gets a whisper that somewhere there's a good set of wet tyres hidden away, he gets his hands on them before anyone else has wind of it. A team-manager is a facilitator. His job is to extract the best from the material, human and mechanical, at hand. Often, that isn't a matter of spending money, it's a question of having brains, judgment and organization. Fundamentally, he needs to be a good shrink.

Alan Rees brought me out of the endless dissatisfaction I'd felt working with Hill and Surtees. The one word that describes 1975 and 1976 is frustration – frustration and anger. There's nothing pleasant in knowing that you're driving among the wankers, or that you have about as much weight and significance in the sport as a driver like Brett Lunger, who would have difficulty getting a Formula One drive if he weren't bringing in money. I don't like having the finger pointed at me and people saying, 'Oh, he doesn't count for much; he only qualified fifteenth.'

The early days weren't all bad, of course. But that's in retrospect. While I was back in that peculiar soup, it looked to me like the end of the world. Some of the anger, being justified, was particularly hurtful. As it was with John Surtees, where I knew that if that team had been smarter and had the management and the application to do the job right, that little car could have been a winning car. At that point, one's anger is vented against a bunch of people who just don't seem to understand what they're doing; it was as though they were not in the same business as I was.

My year with Shadow in 1977 was much less frustrating. Mostly because I knew there wasn't much we could do short of a new car. The one we had was overweight and very slow in a straight line. Nichols and his team were in deep financial trouble and I considered myself lucky, at that stage, to have a good, steady drive. To drive a consistent loser is in some ways better than to have to drive a potentially quick car being ruined by neglect, which was what I had at Surtees.

A season with Shadow kept me in play. Either at the end of the year Shadow would get a new competitive car or somebody would spot me and ask me to drive for a better team. Around the business, people know when it's your car that's at fault and not you. I think I was rated at Shadow by what I could do within the limitations of the machinery at my disposal. 'Look at old Jonesie,' someone would say; 'he's doing well in that old shit-box of his, isn't he!' After all, there's always next year, so my task was to wring the neck of even the worst duds.

There's no over-supply of drivers. If you're good, you'll be spotted. Motor racing doesn't have the equivalent of the great poet dying starving in a garret because no one knows he's great.

At the end of 1977, I signed a contract with Ferrari. That, I thought, had settled my career. I flew down to Milan, was picked up at the airport – with everyone whispering and pointing a finger at me, knowing Ferrari were hiring a new driver – and took the grand tour of the factory. Once I saw their facilities, I just couldn't believe that they didn't win every race: with their own foundry, their own private circuit, their megabucks, where's their excuse?

A.J. had the ritual interview with Ferrari himself, and came away unimpressed. It's not so much Enzo Ferrari's fault, but being a living legend must weigh heavy. Never in the best of health, into his eighties, the old man looks pained by his responsibilities. But there is no doubt that in motor racing, in terms of prestige, there is no name like Ferrari. It is the only car which can pull the fans to a circuit all by itself. In the last few years, however, Ferrari has been adrift of the technical developments

69

in the sport. Back in 1977, when A.J. was signed on, they were at their peak.

I had the usual interview with the Old Man. He was sitting behind his big desk with the mementos on the wall and all the proper lighting on him. To me, he was just this god-like figure known as Enzo Ferrari, and my first impression of him was how very pale he looked; it was the pallor of death. If I hadn't known he was Enzo Ferrari, I don't think I would have been greatly impressed. He was friendly enough in the ten minutes we spent together, but the only question of his I remember was, 'Why do you want to drive for Ferrari?' 'Please Sir, I'd like to be World Champion, that's why.' A stupid question deserves a stupid, if honest, answer.

The accounting department, where we discussed terms and so on, told me that they were after Mario Andretti, but that if Mario wanted to stay with Lotus, it would definitely be my drive: congratulations, welcome aboard, go home and enjoy yourself.

It ought to be made clear here that racing drivers, unlike most sporting superstars in golf or tennis, to mention just a pair of individual sports, are still pieces of merchandise. They are employees bound to contracts, to teams. In the last few years, drivers have proved their independence by breaking contracts: not the most honest or healthy way to handle a grievance. But the choice of ways is not great. Most contracts are annual, but younger drivers especially seek to guarantee themselves drives by obtaining longer contracts. As the competition for good drivers is always fierce, drivers are offered many inducements to leave one team for another.

Monza, or the Italian Grand Prix, is usually the venue for the annual flesh-market, and about one-third of all the Formula One drivers in any given year tend to be either new boys or driving for new teams. The new boys are necessary to replace drivers killed, injured or retiring; drivers change teams for more money, a better car or because of personal dissatisfactions with their current lot. Some changes work, some don't. On the whole, as A.J. says, a driver is better off staying with a known evil and remedying it. Of all the teams to move into, however, Ferrari is the most difficult: the team is exacting, the administration remote, the public fanatical and cruel and the internal politics fierce.

When I heard that Andretti had definitely signed for Lotus, I called up Modena, asking when I should report for work. Ah, Meester Jones, they said, you see, there is this small problem. . . . The problem turned out to be a purely political Ferrari issue: they wanted to boost their sales in the United States and Canada and wanted a North American driver. In fact they got Gilles Villeneuve; I got a telegram through the door saying they were sorry they wouldn't be able to take up my option.

I had already started talking to Frank Williams and I was still in touch with Don Nichols of Shadow. I told Frank I was talking to Ferrari, and Frank said, 'If you can drive for Ferrari, I think you should, because I can't offer you that sort of drive at the moment; but if it all falls through, come back to me.' As for Don Nichols, the conversations between us had reached the point where I had to tell Don, 'Never mind arguing about how much money I'm going to get next year. How about paying me what you owe me from this year?' In the end, I drove out to Frank's factory in Didcot, talked to Patrick Head, his designer, for two hours, saw all the plans Patrick had drawn up for his new car – and knew I just had to join Frank's team. It offered me everything I'd ever wanted out of motor racing: a one-driver team, a light, straightforward car with a good engine, excellent sponsorship and a chance to get in on the ground floor and grow with the team.

Part 3

A. J. Settles into the Formula One Family

In 1977, Frank was still one of the game's all-time least successful constructors. Everyone told me I was crazy and taking a big step backwards in my career. But motor racing is also a business, and good business people make up their own minds. There's no point in asking yourself, 'Have I made the right decision?' You make the decision and then make sure it's the right one. I knew Williams were a good, tight little team. The car had to be better than the Shadow. It was. It should have won races in 1978, but wasn't reliable enough. It began halfway through 1979 and won the Championship in 1980. Which is not bad for a so-called loser and a beginner.

The man who wanted A.J. in his team from the start and who has given him the kind of support that world champions need, is Frank Williams. Frank is a curious amalgam: one half joviality and relaxation – like A.J., Frank Williams has the precious common touch – the other half is rigid, highly disciplined, desperately competitive and like a volcano suppressed. A small, lean, very fit man, Frank made it mainly through sheer tenacity and was not impeded by self-doubt: not any more than A.J. himself. In fact, all three of them, Frank, A.J. and designer Patrick Head, have a sort of intense ego that drives them. And drives them, and drives them.

Here is Frank on A.J.'s early days:

'The first thing I had on my mind when I formed the present team was to find a good professional driver. We weren't over-ambitious; we couldn't afford to be. We didn't go after Niki Lauda or Jody Scheckter: they were beyond our reach, both financially and in terms of their status in what we conceived of as a small, highly-professional team. We wanted work rather than glamour; we wanted the sort of pro who, if the car finished races, would bring us results. A.J. was on the list; so were Gunnar Nilsson and Jochen Mass. All three of them good, solid drivers.

'It was no piece of exceptional judgment or foresight or intuition on my part. A.J. knows perfectly well I didn't rate him that highly when he joined us; I acknowledge that we were lucky he became available at just the right moment. But I had no idea he would be as good as he is. His brief from me was simple: "Don't crash our cars, for we can't afford that many spares; finish in the points and work hard to help us develop our new car."

'I admit, too, that I had almost no picture of his character when he joined us: I'd neither really spoken to him, beyond saying hello, nor spent any time with him. It wasn't until September of 1977, when we started negotiating with him, that I got a picture of his true character: he was as thorough in that as he has been in everything else. And as honest.

'I wasn't at his first race in Argentina, but at the second, in Brazil, he was already eighth on the grid. I was both surprised and pleased by that. But it was at Long Beach that I first saw how ultra-competitive he was. He'd had a bad practice and was seventeenth on the grid, but when the race started, he passed car after car. I remember turning to Patrick and saying, I don't mind if we don't finish; I've had my money's worth, because he's not just a good driver, he's an exciting driver. And I hadn't been excited by a driver's performance in many years. He could have won that race if his car hadn't broken down. But I found out then what he has since confirmed time and time again: that he's the sort of driver who puts in the fast laps you need. He responds best when he's really got to hang it out.

'It soon became obvious that A.J. would be a front-runner and that we'd got more than we bargained for. Being the good businessman he is, A.J. realized that too: at the end of the season, he put his price up. I won't say I didn't mind paying more, but I will say he's been worth every penny.

'As the team has matured, so has A.J.; he's always been a stable character, settled and determined. With maturity, a good driver becomes quicker and better; it isn't merely that he has more experience, it's also that his mental attitude is much more suited to the task at hand and his intelligence begins to prevail over his instincts. There isn't time in running a team, raising its money, overseeing a manufacturing force and maintaining contact with our sponsors, for A.J. and I to socialize that much. I enjoy seeing him and he's always good for laughs. Being in America a while improved his one-liners and he's a funny man anyway; but also a private one, which is perhaps why he hasn't yet hit the public consciousness the way James Hunt did.

'I soon enough found out I had the best driver in the world, the most complete, the most competitive and the most meticulous. He also has this natural force when it comes to driving: he's on the mark from the start, he's single-minded about being best. He doesn't waste our time and I think our job is not to waste his.'

Charlie Crichton-Stuart is A.J.'s friend, confidant, agent: a sort of aristocratic valet-de-chambre. It was Charlie who, meeting a noble Arab in a night-club one night, saw the possibility of bringing Arab interest in motor-racing to the benefit of Frank Williams:

'I remain fascinated by the inner workings of a Formula One team. The public sees a driver, and sometimes the more technically-minded see a car, but though that is as it should be, car and driver being the image of the sport, a Formula One team is an amalgam of so many elements and individuals that just to find your way among the different interests is totally absorbing. It is as intricate an operation as I've ever seen, much more finely-balanced, much more entrepreneurial in the basic sense, than most businesses. In sheer professionalism, it puts any other sport to shame: and has to, otherwise it could not survive.

'Yet, despite the fact that a Formula One team is such a complex operation, it does have a very simple code at the base of it. And those who work professionally in the sport understand it perfectly; they know that their own sense of competition, their own aggression, their goals and private ambitions, are all poured into one man: the driver. Racing may be a team sport, but it's still one man who sits on top of the pile, and that one man is the man who drives the car. Once you've done all you can to put him well up on the grid or ready him for a race, your fate is in his hands. You can't help him any more and everything inside you is represented by that one man.

'All of me is channelled into A.J. I work for Frank Williams, and when A.J.'s team-mate Clay Regazzoni won the British Grand Prix for us, we were all delighted with Clay's win, for we all liked Clay. But it wasn't the same thing, because A.J. didn't win it. A.J. *is* Williams Engineering. He came in with us when we were in the shit and he made us what we are. We didn't feel fulfilled after that British Grand Prix: not until the next race when A.J. won at Hockenheim. That's because our ambitions were on his back.

'A.J. knows this perfectly well. He laughs at us about it. Of course he couldn't do it without Frank Williams and Patrick Head, because we are all interdependent. But the sheer sport of it belongs to A.J.

'I provided the initial contact with the Saudi royal family, but it was Frank who followed it up and made it happen. If Patrick didn't make a first-class car, not even A.J. could win. None of us can operate without the others, and none of us would want to. Each does his part. A.J. could win races without me, but I, too, make my contribution. What I do for him is to be a friend: if there's a bad race, I'm the one he can talk it over with and get pissed with and say the things he can't say to the world at large. With me, he can let his guard down. He knows that I am always for him, that I work to his ends.

'My relationship is so personal that there are races A.J. has won when I haven't even known where Carlos Reutemann finished. I'm proud of that fact. It doesn't mean I don't like or respect Carlos; it simply means I am absorbed into A.J. He came up with us and we came up with him.

'I think my friendship is important to him. He's a lonely man in many ways. He knows many people, but doesn't have that many friends. He doesn't allow it. Maybe everyone wants to be loved, but there are some people who are better equipped to live without it than others. A.J. is enough of an egotist not to care to be loved by all. There are few people whose esteem matters to him. Any summit is a lonely place. There's not much standing room on top of Everest.

'I'm sure A.J. knows that there's not all that much I can do for him. By the same token, he knows that whatever I can do, I will do. I am on his side.

'I don't think he's changed much since he joined the Williams team, because he put his imprint on it firmly from the moment he started driving for us. He did very well right from the start: in Argentina and Brazil in 1978 he reached fourth or fifth, even though we'd qualified well back on the grid. In South Africa, he came in fourth and at Long Beach, the next race, he was already dicing for the lead. An amateur could see he was racing in the most spectacular fashion. His front wing had collapsed, but it was as though that made no difference to the car at all: he was still challenging for the lead, and not just from some indifferent drivers. Reutemann was driving for Ferrari and Ferrari were in a different world from us at the time. I remember us all looking at each other in the pits and saying, 'This bloke's something else.'

'I really don't think anyone in the team had seen how good he really was, but after Long Beach, we all knew we had a potential World Champion on the team. All we had to do was give him the equipment and the back-up and he'd do it: that concentrated us marvellously.

'People don't remember 1978, but that was the year we really began our breakthrough. We were in second place six times that year: that was a year in which Lotus completely dominated the season and Carlos won four races for Ferrari, the ones Lotus didn't win. Our little poxy 06 was in second place six times and there were several races A.J. could have won if the car had been more reliable.

'A.J. was always one to speak his mind. Even back then, when he still had his reputation to make. After all, he came to Williams as a sort of midfield man: not top, far from bottom. He'd won just one race, in the rain in Austria, and we were without doubt the worst team in motor racing. But Alan forced the issue, he pushed us. When things broke on the car, as they did regularly in 1978 and the first half of 1979, he would say his piece in no uncertain terms. He was playing the brash Australian to the hilt. On the other hand, he never made unnecessary dramas. His whole attitude was to do what was necessary, get on with it, and make things work.

'On the first day of practice at Watkins Glen in 1978, A.J. was going through the corner where Jackie Ickx had his big shunt, and his front stub-axle broke. It was a huge shunt, and at 150 m.p.h. He drove back to the pits in a course car, got out on the far side of the pit wall and showed us the front hub in his hand. He lobbed it over the wall to Patrick without a word. But it was the only time I've ever seen the man actually sheet white.

'Patrick Head and I spent the whole night in the Elmira heat-treatment place getting things fixed and tested and when it came to the next day's morning practice, Patrick still hadn't got the car back together again, so we missed the first session. Then came the afternoon session. A.J. went out and put us on the second row of the grid, third fastest, the highest grid position we'd ever had. This was after a 150 m.p.h.-shunt in which he was bloody lucky. He'd had a huge fright. He knew the accident could have hurt him, and he knew it wasn't his own fault.

'More than most, A.J. has the racing mentality: he has the ability most good drivers have, to shut out of his mind what he doesn't want to see. Otherwise, how could he have qualified that high up on the grid at the Glen? His recuperative power is extraordinary; he bounces back to normal as though the untoward had never happened. Most drivers I know would have had the stuffing knocked out of them after that accident at the Glen.

'At Zolder he had brake failure and another big one. He walked back to the pits totally unaffected. He'd hurt his arm but he wasn't even remotely frightened. To be a World Champion, a driver has to have a form of selective blindness. He must remain, against all odds, unsubdued. By mishap in any form. It's the same when the car breaks down. At our first race in Argentina in 1980, when Carlos broke down, he sat slumped by the wheel, his face in his hands and weeping. If A.J.'s car breaks down, he hops out of the car and kicks the side in.

'Frank has always had the ability to run a team. In the past, he simply didn't have the wherewithal. But in a way, the key to A.J.'s success with us is his rapport with Patrick Head. They have more than rapport; they have complete mutual respect. Patrick says that A.J. knows the car like few drivers do; and his personal feelings aren't involved. If something goes wrong, it isn't a blow to his psyche; it's a problem to be solved.

'More than any driver any of us have ever seen, A.J. gets on top of things from the word go. He doesn't work away at his times, chopping them down fraction by fraction: he just goes out and does it. He tends not to practise at his peak, as though practice were too abstract an exercise. That's because he doesn't feel the directness of racing against another driver. His average is the second row on the grid: being still perfectly clear that he can win the race from that position.

'It's the same in testing. We go down to Ricard; it's cold down there, there's nobody about. He still goes all out. The competitive strain in him is so strong that I don't think he can bear not beating a track record if there's one there to be beaten. People tend to look back to a Jochen Rindt or a Jim Clark and ask where are the great drivers of today. I don't think A.J. has a weakness as a driver; he's as complete a driver as they ever were. He is immensely good at racing, and very intelligent and good on the car. He doesn't get involved in first lap accidents. And we were very sensitive about that in the early days when we were bringing Saudis to the race meetings. We had only one car, not two, and if A.J. had gone off at the first corner on the first lap, they would not have been greatly impressed.

'He's the best all-round driver I've ever seen. I don't say that lightly, and it's not just loyalty. The game is hugely competitive, much more so than ever before, and A.J. is on top. When I look back on our championship season in 1980, I realize that A.J. had to *earn* his Championship. It wasn't that he had the best chassis and the title fell into his lap. And yet, he's still underestimated. Which is more than a little his own fault, for he has no appetite for selling himself.'

Constructors, team-managers, engineers and designers vary as much as their drivers; they are in the business for different reasons. Some of them get into it out of passion, some because they were in the motor-racing world as drivers and can't shed their past, some for the loot, some for the glamour. The public knows the driver, but at the circuit, though the driver may be, as Charlie says, at the top of the pile, there is no doubt about who is boss. It is the constructor or team-manager who gives the orders, for it is he who has overall control and responsibility for the success or failure of a team.

For a constructor, the driver is replacable, and so is the car; he himself, however, is the heart of the matter. The egos of constructors show up accordingly. A.J. has no illusions on that score:

No matter how well paid I might be, disregarding the fact that I might well make more money than the man who owns the team, and certainly make more than the designer or anyone else, I am still an employee, and so is everyone else. I have to do what I'm told. Drivers may seem like free spirits, but they have clear obligations. If they don't like what they are asked to do, their alternatives are clear: they can quit the sport, shift teams or start their own.

I have no intention of starting my own team. There is no way, anyway, to run a team and drive. There is far too much for a man like Frank to do. To run a Formula One team successfully is far more difficult and demanding than running a large multinational corporation. In a big company, you can always delegate your duties: you have an organizational chart that shows who reports to whom and why. You have minions and flunkeys to do your business. In Formula One you're just about naked. Each man on the team is naked. If a mechanic fails to put a bolt on properly, it's his responsibility when the inevitable shunt happens. He can't say he was following the orders of the second assistant manager from the left. He knew what his job was and he blew it.

Formula One is a sport, but it's also a big business. It's an almost equal mixture of the two, and as such is at the mercy of all, and requiring different talents from each. It's the variables that make it so complex. There is the personality of the driver to mollycoddle; there are sixteen mechanics each with different skills and different problems; there is the factory staff which builds and repairs our cars, each of them a technician and a specialist, few enough for you to know them all, too many to spend all your time analysing their individual psyches; there is a temperamental designer who knows himself to be a genius, and his staff, who each think he's as much or more of a genius than the designer; there is the meeting of the bills and a payroll each and every month; there is sponsor-chasing, organizing the logistics of carrying cars and people to four continents; there is negotiation with the tyre people, with suppliers of all sorts; engines, gear-boxes, spark plugs, any one of an inventory of thousands – all that has to be kept in your head as well as the main business of getting out on the track and winning.

Frank is exceedingly good at it. Anyone who can run a Formula One team successfully can run any other business there is. I liked Frank even before I worked for him. He was jovial and polite, and I put a high value on politeness.

Civility is very important. Being civil doesn't detract from your inner combativeness or your interior strength. You don't have to be arrogant or rude to be a good fighter. The popular notion of the driver as arrogant, rude, macho and boorish, derives from Jochen Rindt and Niki Lauda, both Teutonic and both naturally aggressively offensive. They set a style: if you weren't rude and arrogant like some Hollywood stereotype of the SS officer, then you hadn't the balls to be a top racing driver. I know what it requires to be good in this sport. I know you don't need to big-note it. A waiter is not a pig for spilling the soup. The world is full of my equals. I like to think I'm the best in my sport and I will do anything to keep myself on top. But the rest of the world remains my equal.

Frank's politeness doesn't get in the way of his competitiveness. As we get closer and closer to a race, he gets more and more wound up inside, but I've never seen him impolite. The truth is that, like myself, he's a very controlled man. But also extremely determined, very competitive and intelligent. He's by far the best man I've driven for. But then I've had some lesser ones, haven't I!

I can only think of one major argument we've had. It was in Spain in 1980 and was entirely my fault. I was coming out of the pits and I dropped the clutch, got into a wheel-spin, ran over a jack and God knows what else. It was all getting a bit fraught.

There was ample reason for the 1980 Spanish Grand Prix to be a bit fraught for A.J. The race was so deeply embedded in the politics of motor-racing that the sport of it was completely lost. It was all part of the interminable FISA-FOCA battle – of which more, later – and the Formula One family was split into two warring factions. The Williams team, hunting the Championship, was among the FOCA loyalists who did race; Ferrari, Renault and Alfa did not, led by Ferrari, who were in the middle of one of their worst seasons ever. The race start was interminably delayed while the wrangling was going on and everyone's temper was at boiling point. In Bernard Ecclestone's loyalist headquarters just before the race, Frank Williams, angry and white, was saying that he didn't give a fig what anyone else did; he was going to race, and legality be damned.

I knew I'd done something wrong and when I came back in, Frank started bollocking me through my head-set, saying I'd been effing stupid, which I had been, and that was no way to prepare for a race. Fortunately, Frank knows I'm not the sort of person to nurse a grudge, and at the end of our set-to, he said: 'All right, bollocking over, get on with it; what's the car handling like?' Thirty seconds down the line, we were both back to normal. If it had been Graham or John Surtees, that argument would have gone on for the rest of the day or for a week. The spark would have gone on smouldering, because they lived by contention. Frank knows his task is to get the best out of me, and he knows that if we have a sulk, I'm not going to do so well. Considering the pressures we were under, with the Championship on the line, to have only one argument is an extraordinary record.

But there are some constructors I might have been happy to drive for in the old days that I would not want to drive for today. Ken Tyrrell, for instance, would rather be a father-figure to his drivers than get on with the more impartial job of issuing orders for the good of the team. He gets too involved and tries to dominate. Rather than seek the opinion of his drivers, he tends to tell them what their opinions should be.

Nor do I think I would willingly drive for Colin Chapman. Colin does not take his drivers into his confidence. I find him rude and aggressive and I like manners. He is a driven man, but in the wrong way: the cockiness and aggro are a cover-up for some sort of insecurity, and Colin is inconsistent. I like someone who is consistent, so that you know each day that he's the same man he was yesterday. Underlying all that is my feeling that he could build stronger and safer cars than he does. Colin's idea of a perfect car might be one that falls to pieces the moment it crosses the finish line. Not my idea of what racing cars are about.

I could probably do one season with Ferrari. There you have a very abstract relationship with the team. You get your memos telling you where to be and what to do, and you treat a Ferrari drive strictly as a job. The truth is, there are just two ways to go motor-racing: either it's friendly and everyone works together as a team, or you're totally detached and strictly business-like. There are some teams that are neither, that fall between the two stools, and there are some teams that are too much one or the other. Mind you, if Frank were doing badly and Chapman had a quick car, I'd join Chapman!

But on the Williams team I get along well with everyone. We don't point accusing fingers at one another; everyone pulls together. Obviously, we have our troubles. We have a standard joke in the team: Frank goes up to Patrick and says, 'Patrick, I want *you* to know we are in the shit!' That gets repeated in all sorts of circumstances. It underlines the responsibility we all feel for each other. Even in our crises, we can have fun. We don't scream and yell; we inspire confidence in each other.

I have complete confidence in Patrick Head. That is the important thing. Both designer and driver have to have faith in each other. Patrick has to have faith in the information I give him, and I know that when Patrick designs a car, he designs one that is both very quick and as safe as he can make it. He doesn't skimp on my life. If he can make a car stronger, even if it adds a little weight, he'll do so. If he builds a new car and I go out testing in it, I know it's not going to break on me. One of the good things about staying some time with the same team is that you have time to build up that sort of faith. I can tell Patrick what he wants to know in the fewest possible words; if I went to another team, it would take each of us a long time to learn each other's language.

The top designers are both the prima donnas and the most sought-after inside superstars of the business. The good ones, like Patrick, or Brabham's Gordon Murray, can be counted on the fingers of one hand. They are the acknowledged legislators of the sport. As they start with a pure idea, something as abstract as a drawing on a scrap of envelope, they live in a much more abstract atmosphere than the rest of the cast of Formula One characters. As one might expect, they are a withdrawn lot. And highly concentrated.

A designer in Formula One does not have a lifetime to make his ideas real; he has a season or less. And, each season, he must not only keep abreast of developments and innovations deriving from other designers, but he must contribute his own share of originality. At the same time, he is bogged down in an immensity of detail which has to do with the preparation and setting-up of the car for each and every race. His world is thus both a long-range day dream and an everyday practicality.

Engineers and designers are odd birds. The engineer lives vicariously: all that he knows about his car – apart from what his intelligence tells him the car *should* do – he derives from what I tell him. He never sits in the car and experiences it. I do that for him.

But engineers are original creatures. Patrick actually gives birth to something new. He puts something down on paper one morning and six months later there is a beautiful and efficient car. He knows everything there is to be known about the technical aspects of the game: the distribution of forces and stress, the ideal aerodynamics, the inter-relation of one part of the car to the other parts. To see this in practice, however, he relies on me. What I tell him about how the car actually *behaves*, as against how he thinks it ought to behave, is fused with his intimate knowledge of the car's engineering, to give him a mental picture of how to correct an error or improve on a positive quality.

I don't tell Patrick what I like about the car; I tell him what I don't like and what is slowing me up. The more intimately I get to know the car, the more help I can be to Patrick. I don't have a technical mind, but familiarity with Patrick's mind has let me into some of his secrets. I like about him particularly that he's as competitive as I am or as Frank is. If anything, he's a worse loser than either of us. If something goes wrong in the factory, you hear this elephantine tread of his, walking the shop-floor or coming up the stairs, boom-boom-boom, and people hide. He has a rotten temper which he tries to control, not always successfully. At the circuit, he's both strict and straightforward. Away from it his mind is in some other world where the rest of us can't always reach him.

With rare exceptions, most sportsmen and athletes in general tend to show a certain distaste for the use of the mind. It is part of a tradition set in the early days of professional sports. In most sports, amateurs held sway; by nature, they were gentlemen and educated. Without the cushion of a private income, they would not have been able to afford the tournaments or events in which they took part. With the rise of professionalism, the anti-intellectual movement took shape. Professional sportsmen became the subjects of films and books, and a distinction grew up between men who thought and men who did, the latter being obviously superior to the former. The attitude continued to hold sway long after its basic premise had been proven untrue, until the anti-intellectual stance dominated totally and became allied to a hard-drinking, hard-wenching image of the sportsman that was totally untrue to those who were at the top of their sports. But the idea of the unthinking athlete persists.

In motor racing the scene is more complex, for the educational and cultural level of different drivers varies almost as greatly as their personalities. The typical motor racing driver is a myth. But the variety of backgrounds means that the general intellectual attainment of drivers varies in almost direct proportion to their parents' wealth and the age at which they took up racing seriously. The earlier they adopted a professional stance, the lower their general level of intellectual attainment: the bug that bites early leaves little room for a formal education. For the same reason, those drivers from modest families – and there are several, despite the financial pressures of the sport – tend to be less 'civilized' in any way that outsiders would understand.

This is reinforced by the huge demands of the sport, its extensive travel, the almost constant work testing and developing and, obviously, by the high tension which surrounds the act of racing itself. For most drivers, 'culture' can only be relaxation. They don't read much except the 'comics', i.e., the specialized magazines which cover their own sport, and you don't find many of them skipping the local disco to go hear Beethoven, though the deceased François Cevert was reputedly a dab hand on the concert grand. Similarly, the works of art on their apartment walls are likely to be middle-class and inoffensive: calm cows and serene landscapes. Their furniture is in the vaguely international style known as Hilton Bedroom.

It is clearly not that drivers are unintelligent, for it would be impossible to get a toehold in the sport, much less be successful at it, without a highly-refined, if specialized, intelligence. But the analytical function, by which they might examine their own motives or see broader perspectives than those encompassed by their sport, is wanting. There is too much doing in their lives to allow for much reflexion. Which may be one reason why books on the sport have, on the whole, been so wanting in any revelation worth having.

On the other hand, drivers are far from being savages. As a collective, they are far better-educated and more civilized than participants in team sports like football. The sophisticated, rootless culture of Formula One, a hodge-podge of different nationalities, different backgrounds, different tastes and educations, rubs off on them. There are no boors in the sport, for a boor would not long survive within the family. Too much, too, depends on their being ingratiating, on knowing how to meet and woo the right sponsors, the best women and the head waiters in the better restaurants. Familiarity with the very rich, with lawyers and the accountants and financiers who make their investments, have made top drivers a sort of special category of the super-rich, and what they do not start out with, they soon enough acquire.

A.J. was a rich man's kid. And a relatively uneducated one, who started young in the sport.

I think drivers do cast themselves in that mould. It's part of the psychology of the game, as though the mind were in some way to be distrusted. I know a lot of people who thought that Ronnie Peterson was as thick as two planks, but of course nothing could be further from the truth: he was in fact highly intelligent, but just didn't care to have people think of him that way.

Some of the reason for this is that many drivers just don't give a damn. A lot of us are just grown-up spoiled brats and would rather play tennis and swim or look at the birds than be made to sit down and think. A big part is played by the press: the I'm-too-stupid-to-think syndrome is an escape from the endless low-level questions they have to face from the idiots who write about them. But most drivers are much smarter than the low-level life they stake out for themselves; for many, that level of life may be a relief from the tensions of driving and surviving in the sport.

Drivers, after all, do not have to sell their minds, or parade their intellects or their philosophy. All they have to sell is their speed. But one cannot drive without brains. No team-manager hires rock-apes: a fool in a Formula One car is a threat to himself and to others. And I don't just mean a fool intellectually or a fool in the racing car; I mean a man who can't think, can't reason, can't grasp what is required of him and can't control his emotions. Constructors look for potential world champions, and recognize that to become a world champion, a very special kind of intelligence is required.

In private, away from the scene, I might show my more intelligent side, but if in general we all look so dumb and only talk about motor-cars and racing, it's because most of us are only doing what is expected of us. We respond to the bores from the press by being boring and stupid.

Most of us, too, are private people. We keep our thoughts to ourselves, and if I wrote poetry, I probably wouldn't boast about it in the pit-lane. We don't socialize as much as people think. I would sometimes socialize with Jody Scheckter. Perhaps because we were both non-Europeans and from similar countries, Australia and South Africa, we got along well. Jody is a case in point. People are always saying Jody is thick. I've always found him clever. But Jody uses that reputation to his advantage. You can't be World Champion and live in a Monaco penthouse on your investments and be thick. He's a sort of uncut diamond. People take different modes of transport to get to the end of the same tunnel. Others have done it more elegantly than Jody, but the end of the tunnel is the same for all of us.

At the moment, I'm so single-minded, I've got attention to spare only for what I'm doing. God willing, if I survive, I'll be a broader human being than I am, for I can feel that my tastes are shifting all the time. I assume that one day one gets to know who and what one is and one settles for that. Meanwhile, it's all change and movement. But more and more I enjoy the company of people who move in artistic circles. More and more I want to meet people who have made it in a big way by their own efforts, like Rupert Murdoch or Kerry Packer, to find out what makes them tick.

I suppose I've grown out of the time when I enjoyed going to parties where people are throwing bottles through windows, or when I laughed at a plane-load of grown men getting drunk and slapping stickers on the stewardesses' behinds. I'm beginning to enjoy talking sense.

For driving is kids' stuff. Full of risks, but still made of a Boy's Own kind of heroism. Which is all very well for boys. But after the first three years or so, and depending on how much progress you make in your career, you find yourself driving for totally different reasons and with a totally different approach from when you started. I know I'm a lot more technical than I was; and, I fear, a lot more commercial. The A.J. who jumped head-first into whatever was going has been replaced by a much more analytical and laid-back self. And that has altered my sense of competition. In my early days, I saw a racing car, I jumped into it and I drove as hard as I could. Half the time I didn't even know what my result was until someone told me. Now, I still want to be quicker than the next person; I still need to feed my ego that way, but I can achieve that same end in a far more rational fashion.

There is nothing new about the rôle-playing of the celebrated. Rôle-playing is one of their chief defences against their fame. A.J. has people believing he's all sorts of things, and he has ample training in verisimilitude, for much of Formula One is a great big con game. The closer you get to the top, the better, the more convincing the con.

Racing drivers have a whole set of standard rôles ready made for them. Some are part of the profession: hero, hard-bitten veteran of the wars ('let me show you my scars, baby'); victims, whether of a bad car, of circumstances, of misfortune. The newer breed, post-Jackie Stewart, the wee Scottish master of the charming con, disguise themselves behind their attaché cases and first-class tickets, as men of business. Their real interests are in buying Lear jets and remote ranches ('how's the Krugerrand today?'). These are always ready with the latest stock market reports, or buy into night-clubs, squash courts, discos. The playboy is a product of the post-Stewart era, of the more photogenic than handsome James Hunt. A.J. can play all the rôles.

It's like playing a great big elaborate game. I relish the rôles. They are a way of getting the upper hand: you know something about yourself which the other person doesn't, and that gives you an automatic edge. It keeps who-you-really-are secret. My favourite rôle is playing humble and Mister Nice Guy. I like it for the sheer return it offers.

Nothing contributes more to results in life than sheer psychology. After psychology comes diplomacy, which is an advanced form of rôle-playing. If there are ten people in a room listening to you, there's a right way to say what you want to say: nine may not agree with you, but they're not going to hate you. Whereas if you say it in the wrong way, nine will. It may be that I'll need those people later on; I don't want a blockade on what I say even before I start talking to them.

Most of the rôle-playing that I have to do is strictly related to money. I have to pretend to like, or to acquiesce to, all sorts of activities that I could easily live without. Money means (besides the team, which pays me a retainer) the sponsors, who pay me a lot more. And sponsors have to have an image of you: hence the rôle-playing. Hence Mister Nice.

The outsider is probably puzzled by the astronomical sums paid by sponsors to buy a few square inches on a car or a driver's helmet or his overalls. But the sponsors are onto a good thing with motor racing. Through television, sponsors can reach up to 500 million people. And as A.J. goes by in the lead, the camera is forced to take in Saudia and Akai, TAG and Leyland. Some 200 professional journalists, plus another 300 locals, cover a race for every major newspaper and racing magazine around the world: presumably their readers use Elf or, in Italy, buy Parmalat milk and eat Parmalat cheeses. Innumerable pictures of Formula One cars appear throughout the world and on fans' walls.

That puts a lot of pressure on the frail morals of the media. Motor-racing is one of those sports where the lines of demarcation between public relations and reporting are, to say the least, blurred. Sponsors pay travel expenses and accommodation; they provide hospitality and gifts. The price is repaid in ink mentioning Goodyear or Elf or any of the 250-odd sponsors in the sport.

But sponsorship is a minefield. Sponsors come and go, coming with success, going with failure. Without them, the sport could not exist in its present form; with them, the costs of the sport escalate constantly until the small are squeezed out by the big.

The relationship with sponsors is one of the less appetizing aspects of the trade. I don't mind it too much, in moderation. It has its own humiliations, particularly when you are starting out. It wasn't until two years ago, for instance, that I found out you were supposed to ring up sponsors and ask them for a deal. I could have used the information when I was starting out; I was always trying to get in by the back door.

Having to go to a party and meet a hundred people the sponsors have invited is no great joy. I make it amusing for myself by picking the rôle I'm going to play: humble Mr Nice or Superstar. Around the business, I find it pays to be a bastard. Give anyone an inch and he'll take a mile. Niki Lauda had it down to fine art: he played at being such a bastard that no one would go near him unless the money involved was really big.

Of course, once you're World Champion, everything changes. Even your friends treat you different. A year ago mates would slap me on the back and stand me a pint; now they don't dare touch my august person. I find that ridiculous. I know I'm not a different person. But being Champion helps business. A lot more people want to meet you. A year ago, if I wanted to meet a managing director, I'd have to explain who I was: I'm Alan Jones. Alan who? Today they say, how about next Thursday?

You can become a 'personality' and have the world forget how you got to be a personality in the first place. We have an Australian footballer who appears on television constantly flogging life insurance and cars. He's so much part of our national advertising life that if he says something is good, the audience thinks it must be; yet probably half the people who believe in him don't know a thing about his career as a footballer. Jackie Stewart's a 'personality' in his own right now. People point him out because of who he is, not because he was Jackie Stewart the racing driver.

It was Jackie who started the whole business for us, being a thinking driver with an eye for the main chance. They had a talking head of Jackie selling Fords at the Motor Show, very life-like, too. But they made one mistake: the papier maché Jackie would pause for breath. That's something Jackie never does. It's a wearing business, being a 'personality'. Once you're at that point, you think you have the world by the tail and you can only think of making money. The truth is, they've got you.

I don't expect to adapt particularly well to my new status. Especially the socializing side: the same boring people asking the same boring questions. One night I was stuck with a desperately boring woman who was really turned on by blood. 'Have you ever had an accident?' she asked me. 'Yes, I have,' I said, 'just last week.' She gasped. 'Going about 250 m.p.h.,' I added. 'And weren't you hurt?' she asked breathlessly. 'Not really,' I answered. 'If you look closely, you can see where they sewed my legs back on, but otherwise I'm okay.' 'Ohmygoodness!' she said. 'What does your wife think of it?' 'She loves it,' I answered; 'she goes racing herself.' I enjoyed doing that to her. You tell them what they want to hear: that you had your head torn off. It makes the sport more exciting for them.

You have to handle the press and the media, because that's why the money's in the sport. I don't have much respect for them. Every writer has his favourite in the sport; that is, when they're not actually paid to support a particular driver or team or sponsor. The press are like the fans; they're for someone and against someone else. There are Ferrari freaks and Lotus freaks and then a huge number of ordinary hangers-on. We get to know them and there are few of them we take seriously.

Sponsorship leads to a situation in which the driver is no longer the sole proprietor of his being. There is an ogre called the public we have to deal with. A lady will barge into the motor home trailing kids and ask for an autograph just before I hop into the car. My weekend is my work time; it's their enjoyment time, and I'm supposed to join in and enjoy myself alongside them. It's as if I walked into their office on a Tuesday and said, 'Hi! how about going out for a drink?' I understand the punters have paid for the privilege of showing up with their anoraks and their beer, but they've got the wrong idea. The sport is work and money.

Their blindness to the pressures we face is largely due to the old image of the sport and the amateur hero with oil stains on his face and a blonde on his arm. It wasn't that competitive in the old days, and it certainly wasn't as political or commercial. Today, for everyone in Formula One, it is a profession, a livelihood, his bread and butter. The pressures are such there is no relaxing, for the only saleable commodity a driver has is himself. Like a singer, he's rated on his performances. But unlike a singer, I'm rated also on how I deal with the public and with sponsors. That's an additional weight. But I still have to concentrate on being at my best as a driver. That's where the money is.

Also, the truth is that it's only the people inside my profession that I really care about. I can do without the public and I can do without the posers and hangers-on. But the people I care for are within the same narrow circle as myself, around my car, my mechanics, my team. The flattery of outsiders is irrelevant; a good word from inside gives pleasure. Ditto with criticism from outside. What do they know about it? But the worst that could ever happen to me would be for Frank or Patrick to say to me, 'A.J., I don't think you're trying today.' I race for the inner circle.

I can also do without the national rivalries and the politics of the sport. But they're the background air we breathe.

Whatever A.J.'s distaste for this aspect of the sport, it is undeniably present. National rivalries form the bedrock on which the political wars are waged. The British like to think of themselves as representatives of the sporting aspects of motor racing; they are also its keenest commercializers. On both counts, A.J. approves. Since the late fifties, the British have had the preponderance of power in the sport: more teams, more support, more engineering back-up, more sponsors participating. For a long while, this gave the British the greatest political weight. But with the influx of more and more money – brought in by ever-increasing costs – that weight began to shift in the seventies.

The motor-racing nationalities have their own alliances among themselves. Basically, however, there is an Anglo-Saxon/Nordic alliance and a Latin coalition. As A.J. points out when discussing his relations with Ferrari, the Italians were always a special case. As Ferrari is a special case. They have fanatical followings, the constructors also produce road-cars and their interests are narrowly private. It is also a fine Italian art to bend the rules to their own advantage: and to do so with savoir-faire. The French, who had long been pathetically weak in the sport – they have yet to produce a World Champion – have recently taken up Formula One in a big way, led by such big nationalized companies as Elf, Renault, Gitanes, Matra and others. The French use the sport in the same way they use the arts, culture, cuisine and fashion: for national advantage, for the greater glory of la France, and to provide the appropriate bread and circuses for a nation in need of pride.

As a man without foreign languages, or even as a virulent and unconcealed Anglo-Saxon chauvinist, A.J.'s attitudes reflect a strong bias against the Latin combination. His heart lies in the Anglo alliance: the British plus the Germans, minor participants today; the Scandinavians, who have not had a major driver since the death of Ronnie Peterson; and the South Americans, or at least those of them whose drivers race in British-based cars. They are what A.J. is familiar with, and hence at home with.

Above left: 1956, Albert Park, Melbourne. Jack Brabham, Stan Jones and Stirling Moss

Above right: Stan Jones and smiling son

Right: 1971. A.J. in his Brabham BT 28

Below: 1972, Airo. All-Aussie racing: Alan McCulley, A.J. and Brian McGuire

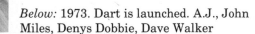

Above: 1972. A.J.'s first F3 win at Castle Combe

Left: Brian McGuire, early partner

Below: 1973. Dart is launched. A.J., John Miles, Denys Dobbie, Dave Walker

Above: 1975, Barcelona. A.J. in the Hesketh 308. F1 debut

Right: 1975, Monaco. A.J. in the Hesketh 308

Below: 1975, Holland. A.J. in the Embassy Hill GH1

Above: 1975. A.J. in a March F5000

Left: 1976, Nurburgring. A.J. in the Surtees TS19

Below left: 1976, Japan. A.J., the Surtees TS19 and the rain

Below right: 1976. Beverley among the YIP hieroglyphics

Above: 1977, Holland. A.J. in the Shadow DN8

Right: 1977. The enigmatic Don Nichols and A.J.

Below: 1978, Germany. A.J. starts fourth

Above: 1978, Monza. A.J. in practice

Left: 1979, Austria. A.J. and Laffite, but it's orange juice!

Below: 1979, British Grand Prix. The unsung mechanics wave the flag

Above: 1980, Watkins Glen. A.J. in the Williams FW0 7B

Right: 1980. The Champion relaxes with Jody Scheckter and Charlie Crichton-Stuart

Below: Patrick Head, A.J. and boss Frank Williams

Team boss, Frank Williams

John Surtees

Ronnie Peterson

Team-mate Carlos Reutemann

Niki Lauda

James Hunt

Jody Scheckter

Drivers' conclave: Ronnie Peterson, Patrick Depailler, A.J. and Arrows' Jackie Oliver

I suppose an Australian should avoid national prejudice, but the politics of the sport push nationality on you until it's hard to ignore. Hatred is a strong word, too strong; but I do feel a genuine distrust of the French. In 1980, for instance, we learnt that President Giscard d'Estaing is able to call up Renault and order them to stop using Goodyear tyres and switch to Michelins. With that going on, how can anyone say politics is not part of the sport? Imagine Mrs Thatcher doing that in England!

The English at least are immutable and still believe in fair play, and that sport is sport, not a playground for politics. The Italians are maniacs; they live in chaos, but their hearts are in the right place. I cannot understand how, with their huge automobile industries, their power, their money and their technology, the Germans and Americans are so under-represented in Formula One. English is the international language of the sport and eighty per cent of the teams are British, but we need the others desperately; our world would be a duller place without them.

Scratch the surface at any point in Formula One and you'll find money. Everybody – drivers, teams, sponsors, circuit owners, suppliers, officials – has a stake in it, and each owns his piece of it.

I know the way my own motivation in the sport has changed. I started out willing to drive anything, anywhere. Now I wouldn't drive a car that wasn't competitive and I certainly wouldn't drive unless I was well paid for doing so. I've done my apprenticeship, I've put in my hours: now, when I go out, I have everything to lose and not very much to gain. I can be blown off the track just as easily in a sports or saloon car race as in Formula One. With my life at stake, I think I'm right to ask for a lot of money; that's the only way I can justify the risk in my mind.

In other words, I don't just do it for fun anymore.

The standard response of any driver to the question, 'Why do you do it?' is that he enjoys it, he does it for the sheer good clean fun of racing. Push at all, and the ground becomes even more tenaciously defended. And the answer is almost invariably accompanied by the statement, 'When I don't enjoy it any more, I'll quit.' James Hunt, for instance, always defended that view: and quit. Out of fear? A.J. has another idea:

James said he got out of motor racing because he didn't enjoy it any more. All well and good, except I'm not sure that James ever really enjoyed motor racing. He was very good at it, but did he have the right temperament? I think towards the end, he was doing it just for the money. I don't think he ever enjoyed it after he won the Championship. And he was right to quit. The trick is to be man enough to say, 'I'm stopping now.' There's nothing easy about the decision. It's far easier to say, 'Oh well, I'll do another season, because then I can buy a new house or invest in this or that.' With James, it got to the stage where he had enough money and could quit, but before he had enough, he loathed every moment of it.

I know many drivers who just can't quit. Either they don't know what else to do with themselves, or they kid themselves into thinking they're still the drivers they once were. And all of them, year by year, dig themselves a little deeper into a hole: a driver gets committed to a way of life, to a certain level and style of living. He always thinks, when I've done this or that, I'll stop. The right thing to do is say: 'I don't care about anything else, I'm stopping. I'm stopping because I want to stop.' But many drivers are like old boxers, and find it impossible to get out of their own little ring.

That rings true. The 'enjoyment' argument has never been altogether believable. Of course there is a sort of joy in driving fast, in doing, even without money, what is forbidden to the rest of us. There's a joy in the intimate connection of man and machine: as with horse and rider, the relationship is almost sexual. And there is the joy of competition and aggression. Drivers are made that way or wouldn't be drivers, and they are as competitive at backgammon, tennis or picking up birds as they are in their cars.

But if money were removed from the sport, how many of them would race just for the joy of it?

Oh, I've been tempted. I see a car or a meeting in the press and I think, it might be nice to have a bash at that. But I can't justify it to myself; it's not a good investment of my one asset, which is me.

We live in a sea of money. Teams are always talking about money, and how they're going to get it. But not all teams are alike in their attitudes. Some teams won't take on a driver just because he can buy a drive. Chapman has sold Lotus drives, but he won't take on anyone who's not a good bet. It's a risky business: if a driver gives you a million dollars, he can cost you that too, in wrecked cars, in inexperience, in lost opportunities.

For that matter, I think all drivers are very competitive about money. I used to drive Jody Scheckter bananas by telling him I was getting $3 million plus expenses. I did it deliberately, knowing he would race less well the next day. For drivers will stop at nothing to get a leg-up on their rivals.

Both money and politics put a great deal of pressure on a driver. If he has weak nerves, it can put him right off the boil; or it can build up his aggro to the point where he wants to blast the whole world out of his way, which is just as dangerous. Charlie says there's nothing so sets me up as a good quarrel at the track with an official! But on the whole I seem to be lucky; I have a relief valve in me, a sort of rev-limiter. I can get myself into a state, but whether I be happy or angry, I never pass a certain level. I live somewhere between top and bottom.

If I'm panicky or nervous about something outside my immediate task in the car, I know it's going to affect me initially, but after three, four or five laps, I'll be back in the groove. The same is true with politics: I can just block them out. The politics is always going to be there in a sport as complex as motor-racing, just because there are so many high-powered interests involved. But now more than ever before I can go my own way; my ultimate destiny has nothing to do with dramas off the circuit but with hopping into the car and driving it.

Despite A.J.'s assurances about being unaffected by politics, he is ruled by disgust rather than uninvolvement. But here, a few words of explanation are needed.

For the past several years, the sport has been afflicted by a long, boring war between two factions seeking to control Formula One for their own ends. One is the 'official' motor-racing estab-

lishment, headed by one Jean-Marie Balestre, a fiery, hot-headed Frenchman determined to exercise the power given him by the rules. Rules which, needless to say, have been codified by M. Balestre and his predecessors. The other, representing the majority of the constructors, is FOCA, Formula One Constructors Association, headed by the tiny, meticulous and shrewd figure of Bernard Ecclestone.

The division between the two is basic. The Paris bureaucracy is top-heavy and not exclusively concerned with Formula One. Balestre's power derives from the Third World and their votes. Ecclestone's interests are exclusively within Formula One, and it is he who truly professionalized the sport. Both sides recognize the need for an impartial administrative body, but Balestre has wielded his power with what seems to FOCA to be partiality. To Balestre, FOCA is simply greedy.

I would rather tell the truth: which is that I don't give a damn so long as I have a competitive car and get paid my money. But people think that a world champion should involve himself and that I should tell the politicians to stop their silly quarrels and get on with racing. I don't think I should have to pretend. Most of us are indifferent to the quarrel. Who runs Formula One, as long as I'm driving in it, is of no interest at all, but that doesn't make the subject unimportant. The public knows far too little about those who really run the sport and, apart from sponsors, who are a greedy lot in their own way, the rest of the people who take part in the sport *have* to think about money all the time. Sponsors and politics are a fact of our life.

At the same time, I recognize that if I just wash my hands of the whole business, I'm being irresponsible. It's like screaming that you don't care about politics and then complaining when you have a dictator. I may just be different. I have this need not to worry about anything outside my own little world. The public wants to hear that I'm deeply concerned, that I'm a fitness freak and jog fifteen miles a day and drink milk. I don't. I hate exercise and love my beer and think about motor racing as little as possible during the week.

But finally the pressures get to me. Prize money – which is where we're getting hurt – is going to be down this year. And that's politics. If I worked in an office and my boss came and told me he was dropping my salary, I wouldn't just react supinely. Nobody would. So I personally despise Balestre for what he's doing to Formula One. To me, he is the man who came in and wrecked the sport I love. He has damaged my income and created havoc in my chosen career. I don't know him personally, but I didn't have to know Adolf Hitler to dislike him. Why should the French run motor racing? Why should anyone run it who is not in it and of it?

A lot of the nonsense is a war between the so-called big marques and the smaller constructors: between Ferrari, Alfa, Talbot, Renault and the rest of us, who just happen to be world champions. The so-called kit-car constructors have won more races than the big boys, more than the big marques will ever win. The smaller teams are the backbone of the sport. They don't make cars by committee, they are not in the game for the advertising and the PR and the perks. The big marques can't put on a good race by themselves, as they could in the old days, when they lined up five Ferraris against five Maseratis.

People demand more of the sport today. They expect good fields and genuinely competitive racing; they want to see twenty-four well-turned-out cars with twenty-four professional drivers. Gone are the days when they'd pay to see ten cars on the grid, five of them works entries and the other five amateurs. All the big marques have going for them is public identification: the fan who drives an Alfa. I'd like to see more, not fewer, 'big' constructors, but not if they think they thereby own the sport.

A.J. often talks about drivers as a sort of medieval corporation, with their own guild rules. And it is true that all drivers belong to the Formula One family in a very intimate sense. They live together and have to go on doing so whether or not they like each other personally. Like all families, Formula One is a hot-bed of gossip. But discretion is part of survival. The man you insult today is the man you have to see tomorrow, the next day and the day after.

As drivers, we face a constant clamour from the public; the public wants us to live and die in accordance with their own ideas of the sport, rather than be ourselves. Every week someone asks, 'Where are the Jim Clarks and Jochen Rindts of today? Where is the purple smoke of Ronnie Peterson?' Ronnie only died two years ago! It's just fashionable to say the sport has gone to the dogs, that it has grown boring and drivers are just light bulbs you screw into the car. Cars have always been important. But in 1954, when Mercedes entered racing for a couple of years and blew everyone off the track, people were probably saying Mercedes were ruining the sport. Now they want to know why we can't bring back the grand old days of Mercedes.

Nothing is more pointless than to compare drivers across different periods of the sport. The techniques of driving today are as different as the cars; they have altered even in my day. I can't understand this endless nostalgia for the past. Or perhaps the public has become jaded, and no longer comes for the same reasons? All it's supposed to be is a bloody good entertainment, a chance to see a good scrap. But the public wants charisma; it likes a certain mystique to attach to drivers. I can only hope that when I've given up the sport, I'll have enough common sense to keep my mouth shut about the people I've raced against and not bore everyone with how great it was in the old days. I hope to watch a race and judge it for what it is, instead of forever comparing it to what I knew when I was driving.

I admit to finding it difficult to talk about other drivers. At the top, there is no substantial difference in style between the different drivers: the good ones are simply doing more and doing it better than the lesser ones.

Naturally, I have to think that I'm the best driver I've ever known, otherwise I wouldn't be doing it. Any driver who is so respectful of another driver as to think him better than he is, is simply a born loser. I have respect for the people I drive against, and there are even a couple I fear as being likeliest to give me a hard time – Villeneuve and Didier Pironi, for instance – but even when I started out, there was no one I looked up to or sought to style myself after. I wrapped myself pretty well in Formula One, in its atmosphere and its techniques, but it was never in emulation of anyone specific.

To be sure, there are big differences of temperament among drivers. Ronnie Peterson was that little bit more forceful than

Niki Lauda, Niki driving more with his brains and Ronnie with his balls; Ronnie letting his back end slide more and Niki being smoother. But that doesn't really differentiate between their skills as drivers. I drive my own way, as a singer sings his own song.

The best drivers are simply the most complete drivers. They are the people who can bring all the different aspects of motor racing together at the right time. They go quickly when speed is called for; they go slowly when they have to. Before they even get into the car, they have set up the best deals for themselves; they are in the right car and the right team at the right time. They can set cars up, they can test, they know how to improve a car's performance and their own.

The best drivers are not necessarily the quickest. There are many quick drivers who never win grands prix. The quick driver who is no more than quick may be able to put together a few quick laps, but he cannot put a whole race together. He doesn't know when to back off to save his tyres or his engine; he cannot recognize when the pace of a race has been hotter than anticipated and that he may have consumed more fuel and needs to conserve what's left.

It's a thinking business. Thought has to be constant. It's not a matter of spurts. When to attack, when to wait, where everyone is in relation to you, all these are vital: the hot-shot gets into it from the word go and half-way through the race he has to come into the pits bleating because his car's been abused. He might win the occasional race, even, but he'll never put together a string of them, and that's what championship racing is about. Similarly, it's no good being a technical genius and setting up a car perfectly and then funk going into corners quickly.

In short, successful driving is about consistency; it is a perfect balance between all the phenomenally different – and severally demanding – requirements of the sport. There is always luck involved in winning: the rivals who eliminate themselves, mechanical breakdowns among others, mistakes at crucial points. From race to race, however, the driver who steers the middle course is the successful driver. Achieving that balance between moderation and analytical skill on the one hand, and courage and aggression on the other, is very much a matter of temperament; and no two drivers are equally good at the different aspects of their trade.

There are some safe generalizations on this score. Italians, for instance, are often let down by their temperament. The slightest little upset, or getting chopped up going through a corner, makes them lose their concentration for the rest of the race. It's something you can play on, as though you were sitting at an organ. If you can make an Italian driver blow his cool, you've beaten him. The French tend to do the same, and additionally suffer from defeatism; that too you can induce in them. It is in these areas that British, German, Scandinavian drivers have the edge in temperament, whereas the Italians, the French and the South Americans might have an edge in fire. But the less fiery the temperament, the more a driver is suited to modern Formula One racing, which is a thinker's craft.

My team-mate Carlos Reutemann is a good example of superb temperament. He has the fire, he can be very emotional, but in his actual driving he also has great self-control. I can't say that Carlos and I have a bundle of laughs, but I have the greatest respect for him. Clay Regazzoni was much more fun to be with, being a great extrovert. Carlos and I get along well enough, but we each keep to ourselves; he does his thing and I do mine. Clay was erratic, which is why he was never truly first-class. But if you have a Number Two who will do donkey work for you, that's all to the good. Carlos won't do it for me, and why should he? He does all right for himself, which is the way it should be. If I were a Number Two driver, my first thought would be to blow the Number One off. It's a cut-throat business, in which we are all individuals and have our own goals, and no favours are asked for or given. We are fundamentally selfish. Otherwise, how could we see a fellow-driver fly off the track and say to ourselves, 'Good, now I don't have to bother passing him'?

My pet peeve among drivers are the ones who can theorize all day but can't put any of their theory into practice. A lot of American drivers can talk their way around a track better than they can drive around one. I don't want to criticize them, for each is doing what he thinks best, but Americans are simply more deeply into bullshit and technology. Give them a new car perfectly set up and they'll shove it through wind-tunnels and a graduate department at a university and have the car two seconds slower in no time.

The French tend to be their own worst enemies. Ligier, for instance, is a very good team: good drivers, good cars. But they will turn up at a track, do a handful of laps in super-quick times and then retire for a three-hour lunch to celebrate. While they're off having their snails and Beaujolais, other teams will plod away, modifying their cars, getting on with their work and catching up. French teams either don't do enough homework or are wildly surprised when someone steals a march on them. Their approach is as professional as the best, but their standards are different. By their standards, they are working hard; by ours they only do half the job.

It may seem strange to the outside world, but we don't mix all that much, as drivers. We belong to the same world and we know each other's foibles, qualities and defects, but it's largely limited to that. The rivalry is perhaps too intense for any real camaraderie. If I play backgammon with another driver, it's to beat him and put him off his feed. The needle is always out.

I knew James Hunt when he was still in Formula Three, and we got to know each other fairly well. I came into Formula One alongside him and he was very helpful with advice and encouragement, which is why I'll always like him. James is the sort of person it's hard to feel indifferent about: people either like or despise him. The more I knew James, the better I liked him. He's bright and good fun. He was also very quick and had big balls. But I didn't join in his outings. I was never part of the jeans and T-shirt brigade. I couldn't stand the entourage climbing all over him, whereas James obviously doted on his celebrity.

Jackie Stewart is like James in that respect. I'm more like Ronnie Peterson: a bit of a loner who did his own thing and had his own interests. He and I had a bit of a wheel-bang when I was in the Shadow and he was driving Ken Tyrrell's six-wheeler. He could have come up to me after the race – he was an established driver and I was a beginner – and super-starred it all over me. He didn't. He came up and said, 'That was a bit

101

dicey, wasn't it?' Ronnie was a great gentleman that way: he did his job the best way he knew and never played anybody up.

Ronnie was never a Number Two driver, though that was his official status when he joined Lotus and Mario Andretti. By half-way through the season, he wasn't Number Two any more: he had made his way up to equal Number One, at least in his own and the public's eyes. He didn't achieve equality through his driving alone. Ronnie knew his tradecraft. He knew the right mechanics, he knew how to connive to get the best for himself. Not the sort a Number One driver likes to have as his Number Two! When Mario won the Championship in 1978, Ronnie went to Brands Hatch and was about a million seconds quicker than Mario. Mario, however, had been with Lotus for some time; he was their senior driver, and when a good car came along, it was only right that he should have his chance to become World Champion. Ronnie was quicker than anyone on the day at Brands, so Chapman pulled him in and made him go out on full tanks for the rest of practice. Being Ronnie, he went out and took pole position anyway!

I've been through the same thing. I was Number One to Clay in 1978 and Number One to Carlos in 1980: quite rightly, the team put the effort behind me. I'd been with Williams for three years and they wanted to see *me* become World Champion, just as Mario was Chapman's designated champion. Number Ones and Number Twos get exactly the same car, but the Number One gets the preferential treatment. I get the better engine; or, if a car is smashed, I get the car that's left.

Ronnie unquestionably should have won a World Championship. I think he was as good an all-round driver as I've seen in my time in Formula One. But it wasn't to be for him that year. He knew it and behaved like the gentleman he was. There were several times that year when Mario was in trouble and Ronnie could have won races; instead, he sat behind Mario and honoured his contract.

Mario is a likeable man, very bright, and has won every kind of race there is. That can't be taken away from him. I didn't like driving for Graham Hill, but I respected what he had done. Results speak for themselves. You can be arrogant, flash or dress how you like: just as long as the results are there. If they aren't, you learn to eat humble pie. I've done my waiting in the wings; we've all done our share. So I don't belittle myself now. But I admire people who stick to their guns, do it their way and still get results.

Niki Lauda and I rarely spoke to each other. I admired his business acumen and the way he built up his image as the machine, the thinking driver. He kept his easygoing side well hidden. He was an unpopular World Champion, but when he came back after his terrible accident, we had to respect him. Was it brave of him to come back? If I had had an accident like his, I might not look on getting back into my car as brave; I might think of it as something I wanted to do. But what you have to admire in Niki is that he came back to the circuits after having already been World Champion. After you've been Champion once, I reckon it's easy just to throw the towel in. Niki had every pretext to quit and he didn't. I have to suppose that there was something left that he wanted to prove to himself.

Niki's temperament was superb. He was always in control: not just of himself but of his surroundings. Fire is an important characteristic, but if it's uncontrolled, it's useless. I look at some newer drivers, like Riccardo Patrese, who are very quick and talented. Most of them will soon learn, but at the moment their temperament lets them down: they make mistakes from their desire to go too quickly all the time. At a critical moment, that desire affects their choice of what to do and leads them into errors.

Clay Regazzoni had a very good, natural, easy balance. He was a dispassionate driver in his last years; all of us become that way as we look on the racing world with a colder eye and recover from our early enthusiasms. Clay was invited by Lou Stanley to look over BRM. Lou was there in his three-acre office and took Clay through his works and said: 'My boy, you have seen my car and my organization – with my team and my factory, we will make you World Champion.' Clay said: 'Fucka the Championship, how mucha you pay?' That's what I mean by seeing things differently when you've been around for a while. For if you've got enough faith in your ability, the only question remaining is, how much? You expect the equipment to be good; the nitty gritty is the money. The more so the longer you've been in the game, the longer you've lasted, the less time you see ahead of you.

The most celebrated, and sudden, retirement in recent motor-racing history came at the end of 1979, when Niki Lauda went out and did a lap's practice in the cold and wet of Montreal and then, telling nobody, picked up his effects, left the circuit and flew his own plane back to Austria. To be reviled by the world's press for not finishing out the season like a man.

Of all the ironies, to say of Niki – who'd gone through fire and hell and survived, and whose face and life had been rebuilt after a return from the brink of death – that he wasn't acting like a man! On New Year's day, when the furore had died down, Niki described graphically how he'd gone out that morning to practise and it had hit him, almost with the force of revelation, that he just didn't want to practise. Not only did he not want to practise, he didn't want to race, ever again. He had better things to do with his life. Asked if it had been a matter of the continued risk, Niki said that had entered into his thoughts, but only in this way: that if a man was thinking of the risk at all, he ought not to be driving.

Since Niki is an acknowledged master of the manipulated story, besides being a mischievous re-arranger of the truth, and since A.J. disagrees, Alan deserves his say:

I'll be accused of cynicism, but Niki quit for far more mundane reasons. I can't say whether he was right or wrong to quit when and how he did, but I have some idea what was going on in his mind, since it could just as well have been going on in mine, or in any driver's.

Niki was a great lover of the V-12 engine. The V-12 engine gave him torque and power advantages over the Cosworth engines which most British teams use, and it was particularly adapted to his style of driving. Niki had started his racing career with Cosworth engines and got nowhere; he'd been a back-marker. However, when he put in some good performances for BRM in 1973 – not getting anywhere but showing enough to be noticed, as we all have to do – he got his big chance, a drive for Ferrari.

You could call that chance: so much in racing is a matter of timing. Either Ferrari got Niki at just the right time to make their cars work, or Niki happened upon a good Ferrari; either way, Ferrari had a V-12 engine and the beautiful thing about a V-12 engine is that you can screw more wing onto the car and still go just the same speed down the straight. You don't have to be quicker than anyone else down the straight, because you know what when the corner comes up and you've got that extra wing on, you've got a whole lot more downforce and you can go through that corner a whole lot quicker. Niki's Ferrari had wings like barn doors. That car made Niki the Number One driver; or Niki made that car the Number One car.

I myself gave serious thought to going to Alfa because they had a V-12 engine, particularly important if skirts were going to be banned. I reckon Niki had similar thoughts. When he left Ferrari – because of the aggravation that seems to attend racing for Ferrari – he chose to go to the Brabham team and drive for Bernard Ecclestone not only because they offered him a lot of money but because Brabham had an Alfa V-12 engine. And if Brabham had managed to make those engines reliable, Niki might have gone straight from being World Champion for Ferrari to being World Champion for Brabham. If he didn't make it, it wasn't from any want of trying.

Then, towards the end of 1979, Niki learned two things. The first was that alongside him he had a very quick young driver called Nelson Piquet; the second was that Brabham was going to race in 1980 with a Cosworth engine. All of a sudden, Niki was thrown into the deep end with the rest of us: into a kit-car and with a very quick Number Two. I don't think the idea appealed to him. Perhaps he was bored; it is more likely that he analysed the situation just as I would, and concluded that, oh-oh, this is looking like hard work and it's not worth it.

But when I retire, I hope it will be at the end of the season. Frank doesn't just retain my services. He hires my mechanics, and they prepare the car in the belief that I'm going to drive it. A mechanic has to think his driver is trying all the time. They are a cruel lot, and if they think their man hasn't got his mind on the job, the car suddenly won't be worth peanuts.

I look back at the old records like everyone else, and think about Fangio's five Championships. I don't think that will ever be repeated. It was simply easier back then. Half the cars were driven by amateurs. Oh, I would have loved to have driven back then! It would have suited my style! But the competition is much, much greater today. Spare a thought for a pro like Chris Amon, who drove for fourteen years and never won a Grand Prix! I started in 1975 and won my first in 1977 in the rain at Zeltweg, but I knew it was a fluke; winning had to be a fluke, in the car I had. I had that advantage over Amon: he was in cars that could have won and didn't; I had one that shouldn't have but did. When you have a lot of near-misses, as I did in 1978, it actually helps you. It made me so impatient for a win, I couldn't wait to get back into the car and turn those near-misses into victories. There are fewer flukes every year. And I'll add, in Niki's defence and mine, that once you've won a few grands prix, or a Championship, it takes much greater discipline and a greater love of the sport to keep you going with the same ferocity.

Part 4

The Profession, Seen from the Top

Driving, power, money. These themes are consistent. Sex, which is a function of the others, is just as pervasive. The groupie is a phenomenon of sports and celebrity in general. Pop stars have them, Mrs Thatcher probably has them. Aged between seventeen and twenty-five, beautiful in a characterless, blonde, laisser-faire sort of way, they are attracted to motor racing by the brush with death, the idea of a hero and, above all, the sheer anonymity of here-today-gone-tomorrow, no-fault sex.

Charlie, I think, put A.J. best:

'His views on women are old-fashioned, to put the most charitable possible interpretation on it. He doesn't believe in women's lib and he's an absolutely conscious, deliberate male chauvinist pig, as are most drivers. For him, most things are straightforward, but few as much so as the sex-scene around Formula One. In that respect, he's your original Aussie: crass, uncomplicated and direct.

'Drivers are that way in regard to women because they are athletes. The edge comes from deprivation, from training, from diet, from continence. It's like a boxer being hungry; the hungrier he is, the better the boxer. The temptation is there constantly, and what the eye doesn't see, the heart doesn't feel. The anonymity is essential, and the girls who hang around are just as much pros in their business as the drivers in theirs: they are the hunters, and the drivers are the prey. They collect trophies.'

Charlie also tells the story of A.J. being interviewed by a celebrated American feminist journalist. The wrong sort of lady to send to interview A.J. She hectored him, trying to penetrate the come-to-bed veneer, and refused to believe A.J. was as simple as he said he was. Finally, desperate, she lunged at him: 'Come on, Mister Jones,' she said, 'there must be something you're afraid of.' A.J., thinking hard and hesitating long, scratching his head as though no fears could possibly enter it, finally did admit to one fear: VD.

Obviously, the sex business does something for most drivers. Drivers all get passes from their teams which are called 'bird passes'. It's just part of the scene. But I don't connect that scene with my motor racing any more than I connect racing with death. Both things are there and would be there if there were no racing at all. But there are drivers who not only use their position, but abuse it. You can see them posing about an extra ninety minutes in their overalls waiting to see what dolly bird is going to turn up. I don't feel any need to use motor racing for scoring that way.

Maybe when I was younger and starting out, I wasn't averse to telling a young lady I met at a party that I was a racing driver. It's a stage we all go through and it does have an undeniable effect on many girls. The girl says, 'What do you do?' And you mumble, 'Mm, uh, I'm a racing driver.' You try to look modest about it, but you know the effect it has. I suppose it's like saying you're a Hollywood casting director or you play drums for the Stones. Today, I'm just as likely to say I'm in the car business. But you know you're disappointing them: they come there wanting to meet a racing driver.

I know some people think sex is a motivation in motor racing. But money is mine, and always has been. Sex is something on the side. Perhaps I shouldn't put it that baldly. I don't race just for the money; it has been a way of achieving something, proving something to myself. Maybe an analyst would say I secretly hated my father and I'm doing it to prove myself better than he was. But for me, it was a goal. Modesty aside, I always knew I would be a World Champion. Even at the low point in my career, when things weren't going well, I'd say to myself, 'Don't worry, you're going to win the World Championship, and that's going to be the one that counts.'

But I live in a masculine, professional world, and I like that aspect of it. I don't ascribe a huge importance to women, nor do

I see why I should change my spots. I am what I am, and contented to be what I am. At this stage in my life, I don't have a huge respect for women. Only rarely have I been able to have a decent, intelligent conversation with a women, and I hold to the old-fashioned view that their place is in the kitchen or in bed. And I know, believe me, how vulgar that sounds.

Yet in the world I live in, women are both a constant attraction and a constant irritation. You can be completely innocent and get dropped in the shit, or you can be guilty as hell and get away with it. I suppose most of us are ambivalent about fidelity and the women we meet around the circuit. There are times when we think it would be best to be married to a dumb blonde who's a terrific cook and won't torment us mentally; there are other times when we're attracted to women who could match us thought for thought. If most of us come down on the former sort, it's because we have enough mental torment during the average day and would rather come home to something sweet and undemanding. I can understand both positions. All I ask is that people be consistent, and when they do make the great leap into marriage, that they should make it stick.

Because I believe in marriage and I believe in it lasting. I believe in families, a fact that has become more important to me now that I have a child. When you're not married, it's hard to imagine what it's like, being married. When you have no kids, it's hard to imagine being a father. When you have both a wife and a child, it's hard to imagine life without either.

Life, however, is the pursuit of pleasure. If you don't pursue pleasure, what else is there? The pleasure of living, of the senses, of business, of getting ahead, of winning. Having children is a pleasure, so being responsible for them and towards them is a pleasure.

I wouldn't want to be misinterpreted. I believe in women; I think they are a necessary commodity. But I don't know if I actually like them. I do find them boring and I do prefer my mates. Some might think I reduce them to commodities because I look down on them: fair enough, you get out of anything only what you put in. But I can't accept women as my equals, because they cannot do what I can do. Nor can I imagine myself working for one. Unless, of course, she happened to own the best Formula One team in the world.

My own wife, Beverly, has been a tremendous help to me. She was my mother's hairdresser and we met on her twenty-first birthday. When I went along to her party, she didn't know who I was, and she stood in the door not letting me in. I thought, What a smart bitch this is! But then I told her whose son I was and she relented. I invited her to go water-skiing and then had a long and stormy courtship with her: off and on, week after week, on for three, off for six.

When I went back to England to get stuck into motor racing, Bev decided to come too. It was off and on again there, but I was going steady with her before I went to Brazil for those Formula Three races. It was in Brazil that I decided I wanted to marry her, which I did in 1971.

I'm not the easiest person to live with, being both moody and spontaneous, deciding things at the very last possible moment, much as I dislike having anyone do that to me. But Bev has been very good; she has put up with all the nonsense, even when we had to live in far from ideal conditions and I was spending all my money going racing when other husbands would be buying a colour TV. She always backed me in my ultimate goal.

She has also been a great steadying influence. For it's good to have someone at home waiting for you, or going along with you to meetings. My home is the total opposite of grand prix racing, and she created that home for me; and I don't think I could have made it in racing without her. But if you ask me why I married her, I don't know the answer. We kept splitting and getting back together and I suppose I eventually missed her: which is not the best of reasons for getting married. But then I think marriage and romance are a question of circumstances and occasions. It's who you meet on a particular day. If you miss that girl, another one will come along who will do just as well. You go with a girl and you get used to her. I'm not proud of that reasoning, but then I'm a sentimentalist, not a romantic, though I suppose I must have married Bev because I love her.

But as for groupies, they're there in any business that has a certain amount of glamour and interest. For the girls, it's a form of one-upmanship. They go back and tell their friends they made it with James Hunt or whomever. I'm dead sure they talk about men just the way we talk about girls. Sometimes for them it's the satisfaction of having a vital connection with someone who's out there racing: for the three or four days of the meeting, the life isn't bad. A lot of the groupies are semi-pros anyway: they're models or on the make, they're in PR, they've got their own hustle. Racing gives them a push and a shove up the ladder. Come Sunday night, we've all flown home. No fuss, no bother.

A connection of sorts between driving and sexual aggression? According to Charlie, yes:

'There has to be a strong bond: if you have to choose one aspect of A.J. that makes him exceptional among drivers, it isn't just his talent, for most drivers have some talent and a number have exceptional talent; no, it has to be his aggression and determination. I suspect that drivers who get enough or too much of it before a race just flatten out; it takes away their aggression.

'Look at A.J. at Montreal in 1980 when the Championship was on the line to be won that day. A.J. looked like he was getting ready to fight the war in Viet Nam, Piquet looked like a gentle little star jockey being lifted delicately into his car. None of us on the team doubted that Alan was going to win that race, even though Piquet had been much faster in practice. To us, it looked like a man taking on a boy.

'But in this as in all regards, A.J. is a much more curious mixture than most people will allow. It takes a long time to get to know him. He has a tremendous defensive guard: either it is natural to him, or he has developed a fear of entering into a relationship with another human being – whether physically with a girl or mentally with a man. I myself didn't get to know him well until the middle of 1980; by then I'd been around him a long time and I'd shared good moments and bad.

'But after we won the Championship in Montreal, A.J. did something quite unlike himself. He came up and put his arms around me and gave me a big hug. It was so unlike him to actually show a feeling that I was completely taken by surprise.

'A lot of his roots go back to his childhood in Australia. He's notoriously tight with money for instance; he gets razzed about it, rewarding mechanics who've been up all night with a single doughnut! Why is this? After all, he's the same man who would, I know, give me anything I really needed right on the spot, with absolute generosity. Well, one reason is that his father went broke, which he's not forgotten; another is his competitiveness – which makes him very wary that someone else is trying to make a fool of him – and his hatred of being outsmarted in general. A.J. gives nothing way, either in the external or the internal world.

'A.J. can lose nine out of ten games at backgammon, but if he wins the tenth, he'll crow about it for hours. Winning counts, and that's accompanied by a positive hatred of losing. I still say he's a typical Aussie in many ways: the son of his father.'

A.J. has no doubts about being Australian: it's in his voice, his demeanour, his love of sport, his aggro, his attitude to the world.

Frankly, I think I'm damn lucky to be an Australian: the old world is falling apart, economically, politically and socially; Australia has just begun to move. It's so remote, we are safe from the aggro. I'm glad that we Australians have the best of many different worlds. I like it that we are a mixture of Italians and Greeks, Croatians and English people. The identification is with England and with roast beef and Yorkshire pudding, but the energy at the heart of us is more American: we like ease, we like technology, we believe in progress. Yet we have the civility of England.

I know that Aussies are thought of as boorish and crude. I suspect that view of us goes back to the forties and fifties when we were desperately trying to establish our own identity in the great old Earls Court tradition of being loud and fighting. Those people are still around, feeding off their old glories. Ockers, we call them; they are our version of American red-necks. The ocker is a working man who gets pissed out of his mind every night; his ultimate vision is a day at an Aussie football game with a can of beer in one hand and a pie in the other. But our ockers are an endangered species. Australians have been travelling a long time now, and they travel young. England is an old culture and the young all share in that old culture and take advantage of it; the majority of Australians now move out and search for that older culture, or rather those older cultures.

But our energy in Australia is spent on other things. Mostly on money and business. We are an entrepreneurial people. Profit and success are not dirty words in our vocabulary; we applaud those who come up from nowhere and make it. In London, if a man is standing in a doorway and someone drives by in a great big white Rolls, he says: 'You bastard, just wait! I'll drag you down to where I am.' The Aussie says, 'You bastard! You wait, I'm going to get where you are.'

I've lived in America and England, but an Aussie has a natural shrewdness which puts him streets ahead of Americans or Englishmen. Some of the best con-men in the world are Australians. But the in thing is to shit-can your own country. A while back, Aussies used to feel ashamed of their country; they went around saying Australia is remote, it has no culture of its own. They bought imported food and imported culture. It was smart to buy foreign, because what was imported had to be better. Then some twenty years ago, we had a revolution of sorts: young people started travelling; they came back alienated from Australian culture; they returned instant experts on nearly everything you can name and they established rules as to what other Australians could and couldn't do. What culture was and wasn't. It was their way of proclaiming that they'd progressed beyond the natives; it was a form of national self-denigration which put them on a pedestal above their ignorant compatriots.

But that revolution led to another: the Australian discovering himself and his own country. That's all to the good, because it is a lot better to be proud of what you are than ashamed of what you aren't. My future is in Australia.

One of the big reasons is that I don't believe that Australia will ever go socialist. I won't have to move. And I can say I love Australia, and that means I love capitalism. Forget about people born with silver spoons in their mouths. I'm talking about the kind of capitalism that says we're all born at the starting stalls and when the gates go up, it's a race to the end, without excuses.

There are very few people in Australia who, if they put their minds to it, could not make it. The examples are all around. It's a young, vibrant country, where entrepreneurial activity is not strangled by taxes or red tape. The Labour Party got in briefly because we were in a recession and the voters grew anxious, but basically Australia is a free enterprise state. We know we're big enough, ugly enough and responsible enough to work out what we want for ourselves. And we look around the world and see that other people don't even have a choice.

For everyone who rises, someone else falls. One man's meat is another's poison. But I have no pity for people who screw themselves up, or drag others down with them. That's why I believe in capital punishment: the man who commits murder has blown his chances to be on this earth. I hate the cop-out. I can't see how, by subscribing to the cop-out, I'm doing anything for myself. Call it pure greed and selfishness. If I don't get anything back, why should I do it?

A complex person, Charlie says. Complex emotionally, perhaps. Living a personal life on the particular razor's edge that is motor racing is always difficult: the pressures on private life are strong, the tensions of public life even more extreme. Considering the millions of pages devoted to the sport, it is curious how little we know about what goes on in the driver's mind while driving. There are aspects, mostly professional aspects, of the driver's psyche that emerge from talking to those who are closest to the driver. But as you listen to Frank Williams on A.J., the good and the bad are weighed up but no attempt is made to sense what it is like to be A.J.:

'A big part of what a driver does lies in his contribution to the technical development of the car. In that, A.J. is in the same position as myself: neither of us is all that competent or well-trained. We both understand the general parameters and we're intelligent enough not to try to encroach on new parameters we don't understand; we try not to get involved with pie in the sky, with new ideas or solutions that are really the designer's province. A.J.'s great value to us is his honesty; he doesn't mislead anyone. He communicates extremely well with Patrick and he has this rare gift of coming to the point, not taking twenty words where one word will do.

'If he has any weakness in racing at all, it is that he's singularly unobsessive: A.J. is with us when he's with us, but when he's away, he doesn't think at all about his car. Carlos Reutemann will call us from Argentina if he thinks of something that could improve his car; A.J. vanishes back into his own world. He could spend more time, mentally, on the job. He is bored by routine. After each and every practice, we have what we call a 'debriefing', in which we go over the car and its performance, item by item. It bores A.J. out of his mind. "How are the brakes?" I'll say. "Okay," says A.J. "No, I mean, how is the brake pedal? Is it a hard pedal?" "Yes," he says. "Hard at all times and for every corner?" "Yes." "How is the balance?" "Oh," he'll say, "the balance is . . ." and then he'll complain. If I hadn't prodded, I wouldn't have got the information we need. It's on boring details that it's hard to get A.J. to think.

'All right, but the racing world is highly technical. We need all the mental input we can get from designers and drivers. We get a lot of feedback from Carlos, even if it's only Carlos needling Patrick. Anything is valuable that keeps the mental wheels turning. The driver is absolutely crucial to that aspect: he is our interpreter, he translates the car for us.

'Of course the name of the game is racing. And A.J. is brilliant at getting cars across the finish-line. He'd rather race people on the track than against a stop-watch in practice. I think he finds practice abstract. But the difference between practice and racing itself is infinitesimal. When A.J. is racing, he's another man. The only men he really respects are Villeneuve and Pironi: he knows they're made from the same mould he is.'

Which A.J. recognizes:

I do race better than I practise, because racing is a form of commitment: once that flag drops, that's it. Practice is not so final. When practice starts, you think you have more time than you do; sometimes it's hard to take practice seriously until suddenly there are only about ten minutes left. But in a race, it's always the same: that night you are going home, and if you don't get a result, you're not going to have another chance tomorrow. There's something important to me about having my

115

back to the wall.

But honesty is all-important. If you're not concentrating particularly well, you should admit that. It is a team effort and you should be giving it your best all the time, but if any falling off is your fault, you should admit that, too. If I have a shunt and it's my fault, I go back into the pits and say, 'Sorry, it's my fault.' Then if something goes wrong that's not your fault, the team will give you the benefit of the doubt. You build rapport with the team, mutual respect. If Patrick tells me my brake pedal won't break under 70,000 pounds of load, I believe him. There are other designers, who will remain nameless, who if they said that to me would make me inclined to have the brake pedal independently tested. The same is true for drivers: Patrick knows that what I say is the honest truth as I see it.

The confidence is vital. A driver is not alone in the cockpit, except in terms of racing; he sits there surrounded by all those who have made the car available to him and prepared it for his race. When we pull into a garage to have something fixed, less depends on their performance; if we thought our lives depended on it, we'd have better garages. In a Formula One team, each member is a guarantor of A.J.'s safety. You could call this 'faith', for that is what it is. It is one component of the mystique of the sport, which has many religious overtones. As, here, A.J. on exaltation.

I can get into a situation in a race – and I can only regret that I have not yet learned how to bring this state of mind about deliberately – when I can get into a real high. I don't know how I get into it; I can't bring it on by an act of will, otherwise I'd do it from the first lap every time! But sometimes on the third lap, sometimes half-way through the race, I get into this high. Then I can drive, on the limit, all day.

It no longer affects me whether it's 140 degrees or 40: neither temperature nor any other outside circumstance is of any consequence at all. The feeling is fantastic. My concentration is 1000 per cent; I enjoy every second of what I'm doing; I lap superquick. It's a form of euphoria. Nothing can beat me and I can drive like that all day until I run out of fuel. The race seems to go very quickly: before I know it, the pits are hanging out a sign saying ten laps to go.

There are other races which seem 500 laps long. I ache and think, 'Oh God! I wish this bloody thing would come to an end.'

Luckily, races like that are a minority. In most, I seem to get into a groove, and when I'm in that groove, I can go on forever. I wish I knew how I got into that state. I don't. I simply find myself in it. I don't sit there saying, 'Ah, here comes my groove'; at some point I'm just in it.

Then I drive out of that window in my helmet. I look through that window and what I see out of it is the sole and only thing that exists in the whole wide world; everything is happening out there in front of me. My legs and arms and every other part of me are just parts of a whole and doing what they're supposed to be doing automatically, so that I don't have to think consciously about gearing or braking or accelerating; that's all going on without any orders from me. I concentrate, intensely, on everything that's in front of me: be it a car or a corner, there's an invisible line extending from that window in my head to whatever's next. My body is in unison. It doesn't really exist; it's compacted, the whole of me is bunched up tight inside that little area of plexiglass. I'm entirely in my helmet and I think of myself as being the helmet, looking out. Everything, body or car, obeys that module.

The sensation is not physical. Nor is it the tunnel vision so many drivers talk about, which is to block everything *else* out of your mind. I don't feel I'm missing anything. In fact, I'm seeing more than I ever have before. My vision is enlarged and the sensation is purely mental.

It is something like rhythm. I love to get into the rhythm of a circuit. There are times when you get into that rhythm and stay in it all day, as though you were part of the flow of a current. I change gears, I brake, I turn: always in exactly the same spot, lap after lap.

Then there are times when I cannot get into that rhythm at all. Whether I can or I can't is not a matter of a particular circuit, nor is it the product of any other constant. That's why I think it is a state of mind. And if I can't get into it, it's because that delicate balance in my mind has been upset: usually by

117

some idiotic triviality, a bad breakfast, running late, an argument, anything.

Getting into that high is a matter of ritual, of mental preparation, of being in the right state before going out. As when the bullfighter goes down to the plaza three hours before the corrida, always solemn, doing everything in always the same order, surrounded by attendants in the same state of sober concentration. It is the kind of concentration which makes a higher awareness possible. Prayer and fasting did it for saints.

I like to get to the circuit at least an hour before I have to get into the car. I hop out of my road-car, I go for a brief walk, I settle myself down. I like to have plenty of time. I like to talk to Patrick, amble up to my race car and get on with it.

Usually, I drive to the circuit with Charlie. Charlie's mood never varies. He's always pleasant and good-humoured and usually makes me feel the same. We talk any old nonsense and after a while, nothing seems to matter. We arrive early because, though Charlie claims nothing sets me up like a good argument with an official, the truth is I dislike last-minute hastles.

Most drivers have a routine of a sort for race-day, even though they're not always conscious of it as a routine. It's like the routine of going to bed when you're a child: now I lay me down to die.

I have one of those little alarm clocks and I allow a good hour from the time I wake up until the time I leave my hotel room. That hour is to allow me to piss about and not feel hurried or pushed. I get up, have breakfast in my room, play a little bit of music, or, if I'm in America, turn on the telly and listen to the news, read the paper and so on. That's why I'm happiest in countries where they speak English; I feel at home. Then I have my bath, shave, and meet Charlie or somebody else from the team down in the foyer.

The calmer I keep myself, the easier it is for me to get into my rhythm. There is definitely a ritual to my actions. I always use the same after-shave and I'm always very clean-shaven. If you feel clean, tidy and neat, you'll drive cleanly, tidily, neatly and smoothly. If you need a shave, your hair is all over the place and you've got dirty fingernails, I believe you'll have a messy race. I always wear red underpants. The red underpants are a good-luck thing, but the shaving and the after-shave is foresight: if ever I have an accident and I'm taken off to hospital, I want to be close shaven and smell nice.

The state A.J. describes is not merely manic, but also obsessive in its repetition of minor details to get a special effect. Writers, who are intolerably affected by the size and colour of their paper or the quality of their writing instruments, are not very different. It is like Bjorn Borg's obsession with the pressure of the strings on his racket or a football player who must emerge onto the pitch through the players' tunnel either first or last.

Once I'm at the circuit, I go and see and talk to just about everyone on the team. I say hello, have a cup of tea, walk around and get back into the atmosphere of the circuit, from which I've cut myself off the night before. I get changed in the motor home and amble across to the car some ten minutes before it's time to get to work. I get in very calmly, go through whatever Frank or Patrick want me to go through – there might be two cars set up differently and they want to try something out – and then after practice, there is the de-brief, after which I enjoy a lot of nonsensical talk and wind myself down.

I don't like to talk deals or anything heavy at the circuit. And during a meeting, I find that I will build up tension from the first to the last practice session. The last session is timed and subconsciously a driver gets himself worked up for that one. That's when the watches are on you and when you set yourself up for the race.

After timed practice, I often find I'm a little bit light. That's an odd feeling: light and removed, distant, perhaps a bit spent. I generally stay another half-hour at the circuit doing nothing in particular. Then I like to get back to the hotel and relax. I watch the telly, swim, go shopping. Because I like to get back to a normal environment fairly quickly: like getting a rubber band that's been stretched to come back to its original shape. There is something called 'feeling normal', and racing is not a normal activity. I like the normal, the regular, the known, the usual. I like to get back into my civvies and rejoin the human race, have an early meal and get into bed, preferably by ten.

A little 'light', a little 'spent': the driving is over for another day; the driver is still there in one piece. These are not conscious thoughts. But the relief, the freedom, the sense of a return to normality, indicates clearly enough a realization of the extremity of the act of racing. For all that drivers claim to 'enjoy' racing, it requires the screwing tight of the mind and the body. The activity goes against the grain of body and mind: hence the preparatory ritual and the post-racing let-down.

On Sunday night, after the race, it is a more extreme version of the same thing. I feel very light, very relieved, very happy: unless of course I've had bad luck or a bad race. Ninety per cent of the time I'm just relieved the race is over. I go into the motor home and have a few beers; and I find I eat and drink and talk a lot more after a race. It's part of the winding-down process.

Having said that about routine and calm, there have been times, particularly in my Championship year, in 1980, when I got angry and still went well. Especially at Zolder, where my race-car broke down. After that, I went storming back into the pits and wanted to get into the spare car, but Carlos was out in it. I was storming up and down and so keyed up that Frank asked Carlos to come in. He put a brand new set of tyres on the car for me with ten minutes to go in practice.

I was pissed off at everything: at Carlos being out in the spare, at being only fourth quickest, at nothing going right, at having the whole world against me. I got into a manic state. When Carlos brought the spare in and Frank had put the new tyres on, I got in and drove eleven-tenths for the last three laps of practice and got myself onto pole. And with that, all my anger vanished.

To get into that state, it's easier to have everything working auspiciously for you. It's easiest of all when I'm leading the race, when there are no dramas with the car and I just feel supremely comfortable and confident. Either that, or getting away from another driver and chasing one. Those are good conditions to be in. The first twenty laps are the ones that make or break you. Every little gear change, every braking marker, everything counts. Miss one and you're going to go slower. Get it right and see out of the corner of your eye in your mirror that you've picked up a length, and you get your reward: you've gained something and your opponent has lost something. Gaining something is a very good feeling.

Out of those accumulated good feelings comes confidence and, ultimately, infallibility. A tennis player in that state can pull off shots that doubt would inhibit. When the difficult has become a piece of cake, the driver is no longer wrestling against the machine; he is freed from all restraints. It is a form of knowledge.

There are meetings I go to at which I feel very relaxed and very confident beforehand. Sometimes I know on a Thursday or a Friday that I'm going to win that race on Sunday. At the end of 1980, when the Championship was up for grabs between Nelson Piquet and myself, I knew I was going to have a good result. At Montreal, everything was at stake, because I was running out of time; somehow, because there were only two races to go, I felt absolutely relaxed and confident.

I thought I had Piquet's number. To tell the truth, I thought I had everyone's number in Montreal. The only thing that confused me is that I was quickest in the first day's practice, both morning and afternoon; I was quickest again on the second day in the morning, and then in the afternoon, Nelson went out and blew me off the track by about a half-second. He found a second-and-a-half somewhere, and that stunned me. I wondered where they'd found that time, but we have a hypothesis.

There is another area of competitiveness that is shrouded in mystery. Legality in motor-racing is based on the Yellow Book, which contains the rules that define all the formulae in motor racing. Within those limits, or by finding loopholes in them, teams will do anything at all to find that little extra time A.J. is talking about. The tricks employed are often unverifiable. The smart team is the team that doesn't get caught with its hand in the cookie jar.

121

There are people who say that Nelson had a 12–1 compression ratio engine in his car that practice session. A 12–1 compression ratio would have given him a lot more horsepower, but it has this defect: it needs an additive to work properly, and additives of any sort are of course prohibited.

The next morning, race day, during the warm-up, I was quicker than Nelson in his race-car. At the start of the race, I outdragged him, and then we touched. That caused a re-start of the race and as Nelson's race-car was damaged in the shunt he had with me, he had to use the spare. Well, he went out on the second start, he passed me, he passed Pironi as though we were both parked. But a few laps later he'd burned out his pistons. There are many reasons why pistons burn out, but what if they had left the 12–1 engine in the spare? They couldn't have put additive in the tank because if he had lasted out the race and there had been a fuel check, Nelson would have been disqualified. So they would have had to fill up his car with normal fuel. And that would have burned out his pistons.

Brabham would deny it and I'm certainly not suggesting that is what happened, but it shows how suspicious people can be in this business. It is also said that you can't do a thing in Formula One without someone finding out sooner or later. The 12–1 compression engine isn't illegal; the additive is. To be honest, I'm all for it. As long as you're not actually cheating – or even if you *are* cheating and you don't get caught – anything you can think of which is going to give you a little extra edge is worth doing. A. J. Foyt is a case in point. Straight after practice he drives his car back into a locked garage and he won't let anyone in there. That's what racing tricks are about: thinking them up in the first place and then making sure you're not caught in the second.

Part 5

The Whole Complexity of Life

Drivers are subjected to many different kinds of pressure. Often, it is the outside world which impinges, and nowhere was this more true than at Zandvoort in 1980. Drivers are a superstitious lot, and A.J. faced one of the worst hexes of all: the belief of others that the World Championship was his for the asking.

Winning the Formula One World Championship is perhaps sport's most taxing individual enterprise. It is no one-shot, but a long season in which a whole team must be bent to the same aim, and in which attention and concentration must be kept constantly at the maximum. To become Champion requires scoring enough points in each of the fourteen to sixteen races in the average season to finish ahead of all others. Because of the rules, the points for the various placings – nine for a first, six for a second, four for a third, and three, two and one for fourth, fifth and sixth places – have to be reasonably evenly distributed between the two halves of any season.

A.J.'s 1980 season had not been one of easy domination. He began well, winning in Argentina; he stayed on top in the standings by taking third place in Brazil, a race which Rene Arnoux won for Renault. For the next three races, in South Africa, Long Beach and Belgium – for his win in Spain was not allowed to stand for the Championship – it was Arnoux who led the tables; and though A.J. finally recaptured the lead with a stunning race in the French Grand Prix at Ricard, he later had to wrest it back from Nelson Piquet, who had forged narrowly ahead at Monaco.

By Zandvoort, in late August, three straight wins by A.J., each of them ahead of Piquet, had put Jones in front by eleven points. Eleven points is not exactly an impregnable lead; it is the sort of knife-edge when a single slip-up or a sudden win by your adversary can reverse the rôles.

123

'A Different Being'

At Zandvoort, which Piquet won and where A.J. did not finish in the points, the rôles were indeed reversed. At that point, A.J.'s victory in Spain weighed in everyone's mind: what if he were denied his Championship by the politics of the sport? At Zandvoort, A.J. was snappy, on edge, intractable.

I was highly annoyed at everyone's presumption. Goodyear wanted me to sit up on a pile of tyres with my thumbs up, getting their advertisements ready for the next year. I kept on telling them they were being ridiculous; 'If I don't finish the race and Piquet wins,' I said, 'that's going to make the race very, very tight.' And so it transpired. Perhaps because I was thinking of the possibility, because it was making me nervy. I could see all the Goodyear people tearing up their photos and their copy and replacing me with Nelson Piquet.

In this game, as long as anyone is in with a mathematical chance, nothing is really over. So many things can go wrong. I knew I wasn't champ, but the rest of the world didn't seem to want to recognize that fact. People would come up to me, and say, 'Hello champ!' and I'd glower at them. They weren't thinking; they didn't realize they were putting extra pressure on me. If I didn't become Champion, the same people would be saying, 'Oh, old A.J. really blew that one, didn't he!'

A driver creates his own pressures. But he is the best judge of what is weighing on him and how to cope with it. That doesn't prevent many drivers from making something out of nothing and making additional pressure for themselves. We come in different types. There are philosophical drivers who take things as they come; there are others who will hit the roof at the drop of a hat. Even the calmest driver will have a day when things upset him that normally wouldn't at all. The strain is in trying to be the same person every time you're on the track.

The sort of person I am on the track, however, is totally different from my other personality. On the farm, any resemblance between myself and a racing driver is pure coincidence. But when I get up and have to race that day, I'm a driver again. I approach my whole day differently. I am, literally, a different being.

124

I think that's true of everyone in the family. I never see it, of course, but Patrick and Frank put on a little show of their own during every race. They snap at one another. Patrick will say, 'How's he doing?' And Frank will snap back: 'I'm not in the car with him, how should I know?' At Montreal in 1980, Patrick went and sat inside our garage; he couldn't stand actually watching the race and being powerless to affect its course.

Montreal will always be questioned by some people, but my version of it is the truth. I outdragged Piquet at the start and, as far as I was concerned, I was in the lead and had the right to choose my line. If you get even half a wheel in front of someone else, you have a right to take your own line; it's up to the man behind to look out for you. If I'm behind someone – it could be the slowest driver on the circuit or the fastest there is – and I try to outbrake him, or slip through some esses on the inside and he cuts me off, that's his right and it's up to me to back off. If you look at a replay of Montreal, you'll see that Piquet did exactly the same thing to Pironi, only Pironi had the brains to back off. He knew there were another seventy-five laps to go and that nobody wins a grand prix on the first lap.

So far I've never had a start-line or a first-lap shunt. If it's a gamble, bugger it, let the other man through: there's always time left to have a go at him. If you're in the last five laps, that's different; then you have to have a big, aggressive go at him. But early on, you have to say to yourself, 'Frank didn't fly the car and all those mechanics all the way to Canada for you to wipe the car out on the first corner.'

Aggression is necessary, but uncontrolled aggression won't help anyone win grands prix. Yet despite the fact that every driver knows this, there are still some drivers who seem prone to accidents. Sometimes an accident has to be a mix of lack of skill and the wrong temperament. Look at Jean-Pierre Jarier in Interlagos a few years ago: he had a five-hour lead in that race and still went off. If all the cars had spun off where he did, that would have been different. But he was the only one and someone else won that race.

If my lead is big enough, or if I have any doubts or queries of any kind, I back off. I'll have put a lot of effort into building that lead, and I know if I need to, I can always build it up again. To win a race by two seconds is as good as winning it by forty. There were many races in 1980 where I backed off and did slow gear changes; I knew that whoever was lying second could get close to me, but the car had enough to rebuild the time I was losing. I concentrated instead on conserving the car, not over-revving it, not wearing out my brakes or tyres.

If I had been challenged, clearly I would have thrown caution to the winds, but if it were just a matter of getting into the car and going quick, there'd be a lot more drivers up around where I am. The smart driver plays each lap as it comes up, and the really good ones win races in the slowest times, not the quickest. Unfortunately, I dearly love having a go. Nothing pleases me more. Psychologically, I don't like being on pole. Inside me, I think I prefer being on the second row so I can work someone over. It's a justification for driving that little bit harder until I take over the lead.

I happen to remember every race I've ever driven in. Sometimes my memory has to be jogged, but once that happens I can re-drive the whole race from start to finish: I get back in the car mentally and do the whole thing. And if you ask most drivers to talk you through a lap, you will find that they take exactly as long to talk you around that lap as they take to drive it. That's how vivid it is; they relive it as they're telling you about it.

Necessarily, you have occasional run-ins with other drivers. I've never actually whacked one, but I've been mightily tempted to do so. I had a set-to with Bruno Giacomelli at Long Beach. I had been behind him for two laps, but I was a full lap up on him. He knew he was being lapped. In that situation, a driver should make it easier for you to pass. Bruno knew Piquet was leading the race, because Piquet had just gone past him: he could either screw me or make the whole thing neutral by moving over. I tried to outbrake him, and he just turned into me. I had a go at him after that and brought it up at the drivers' meeting.

De Angelis did the same thing once. I had left my braking too late and had to scream off up the escape road, which happened to be the entrance to the pits. Afterwards, I apologized;

I thought I might have screwed up a good lap for him. It was my fault; I'd left the braking too late. When I said I was sorry, he questioned my motives. He said, 'Are you sure that's what happened – you just left your braking too late?' That was like a red rag to a bull. If I had the decency to apologize, he ought not to have questioned that; if I hadn't been sure it was my fault, I wouldn't have apologized.

These are the pressures that derive from the extreme competitiveness of the sport. I am constitutionally incapable of getting into a car and being jovial and relaxed. I once drove for Teddy Yip, one of the world's more colourful characters, at the Macao Grand Prix. I did it for the sheer fun of it, knowing that his cars are often a shambles. So I was having fun before the race started; but once I got into the car, I started coming to the boil. I cannot just take it easy or say that it doesn't matter that there are a dozen things wrong with the car.

Perhaps my ego won't allow me to do that. I have to be the quickest, I have to be best. If I'm not, and I think it's because of poor equipment or organization, I blow my cool. And if I haven't been putting out, I think they're perfectly entitled to have a go at me, too. At least that way I'd know they were as serious and as determined to get results as I am.

Of all the aspects of motor racing that the public has in its view, the start of a race must always be the most memorable and directly exciting. With a grid, usually, of twenty-four cars, the noise, the build-up, the tension, the anxiety, the sheer spectacle, make it one of those few moments in the sport which the driver shares with his audience. He and they must be, one thinks, sharing the same thing.

I've watched racing from the outside. I know how exciting the build-up can be, and that mad explosion of power and noise when the light goes green.

For a driver, the sensation is very different. The driver is not watching the start, nor watching himself as a starter; he is concentrating, he is composing his mind. I have walked to my car, I've got in, and once I'm in, I know I won't get out again until the race is over. My effort in the car is to try to relax, so

127

that when the five-minute board is shown, I am completely at ease. The greater the tension, the greater the need for calm.

I play a game with myself. When the five-minute sign comes up, I say '*cinque minuti*' and start counting down, or just counting, in all sorts of languages. It is a deliberate form of distraction from what is going on around me.

The start itself is neither joyful nor frightening. It is a commitment. I am there because I chose to be there. I do not sit in my car wondering what I'm doing there or wishing to get out; nor do I think, 'Gee, this is great, I'm really enjoying this.' I simply go through whatever is necessary to get the best result. And that means going through a drill with myself. For instance, I try to leave the car in neutral for as long as I can, because if a driver puts it into first too soon and keeps blipping his accelerator, the clutch will burn out. There are a hundred little things like that to think about that help distract the driver from what's at hand or around him. By going through a drill, I am actually starting the race before the light turns green.

Mentally, I am thinking all the time, What might give me an advantage? At the re-start of the race in Montreal in 1980, for instance, I drove back to the start-line and made sure I had my car sitting exactly on the tyre marks I'd left from my first start. There, I knew, there would be more rubber on the track, and when I dropped the clutch, that little extra bit of rubber would give me better traction and a faster start. Piquet drove up and put his wheels between his tracks. I got the better start. At Brands Hatch, because the circuit runs at an angle, I point my car slightly uphill; when I drop my clutch, the car corrects itself.

As the outsider might gather, the start puts a terrible strain on both car and driver, and it's my job to keep that strain to the minimum. I leave the car in neutral until the red light comes on; at that point I still have ten seconds to get into first gear. If you don't get excited or flustered, that's plenty of time. The five minutes of waiting for that first positive act – getting into gear – feel like a month. Like everyone else, I tend to think I've left getting into first too late. The truth is, it's a fine line between over-revving, which will wreck your clutch, and under-revving and stalling. By the time you've thought through all the variables you ought to have checked out, there's little time to have butterflies.

I spend that long five minutes, for instance, taking careful note of where the other cars are, and trying to see who's where and guess what he's likely to do. My aim has to be to outguess them. I think, behind me is so-and-so, he's going to try to scream up between myself and the wall; so I move the car fractionally closer to the wall to close up the gap.

I don't check the drivers in front of me before the start. I simply concentrate on the lights. It's like keeping your eye on the golf ball: you're not supposed to be looking where you're aiming, but at what you're hitting. Of course, as soon as you line up your car, you take note of where you'd like to go. In every start, there's a sort of ideal position to be in. And, as soon as the lights change, my eyes come right off them and I go as fast as I can into the position I have decided to take up. If I feel I've done a good start, but I'm aware that someone behind me has done an even better one, well that's his bad luck: I put my car where it's going to make him wait.

But a start is forever fluid. Someone else may have taken up my position or be in an ideal position himself; in that case, I have to change my plan, and my mind, very quickly indeed. And that happens often enough, God knows! There will be two cars in front of you, and that gap that you wanted to shoot suddenly closes; well, you'd better change your mind quickly and head outside.

Knowing what you can and can't do is instinct. A good start simply means one in which you've got into the position you chose. If you are heading for a gap between the two cars ahead of you, you must actually be there already, so that they can see you out of the corners of their eyes and can no longer shut you off. The tyres are wide, the cars are quick: to pass someone or sneak through a gap is not a matter of speed, but of spoiling your opponent's manoeuvre. You have to position your car in such a way that he is the one who has to yield. When he backs off, you automatically get that little extra bit of speed that enables you to overtake him. You've taken away his line and established yours.

From the outside, a start may look like an almighty scramble.

From the inside – at least in my day, when we are lined up only two abreast – it is not so different from being on a motorway. The track is about three lanes wide and nothing obstructs your vision. What is more difficult is making the instant decisions which someone else's move may force on you. I've gone for lots of gaps that have closed up, and I've also been blocked and seen a gap open up before me. Suddenly there's this great big space in front of you and you can drive right through it! Afterwards, people say what a great start you made, but in fact it was just easy.

A driver has just enough peripheral vision to make this sort of decision. I work on the theory that if I can't actually see them alongside me, then they're not there. If they are a quarter way into me, they don't exist; if they're alongside me and I can see them, they are there. Even at the speed we're going and with all the confusion of a start, you can always sense another car alongside your cockpit.

Just their presence, however, doesn't mean that I'm going to give way. I can still try a bit of bluff and pretend I'm going to take my own line regardless. It quite often works. The bloke thinks, 'Christ! he hasn't seen me,' and it's he who backs off. But the good drivers stick to their guns and if you see another car in the middle of your cockpit, you are the one who is going to come off second best if you touch.

I'm aware that I'm playing it all down, and that the truth is just a little different. Of course you are surrounded, of course you may be scared at a start, but, being in that manic, committed state, I am so hyped up, the competitive edge is so sharp, that I know I am going to have a go, regardless of the risk. I am aware of a mental change at the start, but I don't feel any different physically; if anything, I get steadily calmer. I feel like a pilot. He takes off and then there's nothing but him and the wide blue sky. The same holds in a racing car. The road is all mine. No Frank, no Patrick, no mechanics, no other car on the grid. No one, just me. I'm the master of my own fate.

I've had races entirely without jubilation or excitement, even though I've won. That's the difference between a race seen from the inside and the outside. At such a race, people will think you've driven beautifully, but no, it's the car that's behaved beautifully, the handling that's been perfect, the engine that has held up. And on occasions like that, you know in your heart that anyone could have done what you just did.

Then there are other times when you've driven your balls off and come in third. I might feel tremendous inside. Until someone comes up and says, 'Well, what was wrong?' The disparity between what I know and what other people perceive about my performance is the reason I am reluctant to pass judgment on other drivers. Only the man in the cockpit knows what is going on; he's the only one who knows whether he could have wrung more out of his car on that day.

The actual technique of driving, what a driver feels or does out on the track, is seldom talked about. They are part of the inner lore of the sport, and not transmissible even from one driver to another. They must be experienced.

If you could imagine sitting in the cockpit with a Formula One driver, you, like almost anyone else whose experience has been limited to a road-car, would be both exhilarated and scared out of your wits. Probably more the latter. What I do and the speed at which I do it seem to be absolutely routine. That is because experience has made me relaxed, and relaxation is what makes your skills emerge. He who is frightened or tense at the wheel is going to be drained.

When I was learning to fly in a Cessna 150, a plane most pilots consider a piece of cake, I would hop out of the plane sweating; ten minutes was like a whole grand prix, and I was all white knuckles and tight muscles. I just did not have the control over that plane I thought I should have. My concentration on getting that control was such that it just wore me out. I've seen the same thing on the track. I've seen drivers who've had to be literally dragged from their cars after ten laps, they were so knackered. It was the white-knuckle syndrome. The hands gripping the wheel, trying to squeeze right through the gears.

How can you do two hours in a Formula One car at 120 degrees? Only by experience. Put a fighter pilot in that Cessna and everything would seem to him to be happening so slowly that he would be utterly relaxed. Relaxation leads to calm in assessing the situations you have to face; tension makes you over-drive and over-brake.

Of course, if you're in a bad car or at the back of the field, it's much harder to relax. It's a vicious circle, like a football team that's not playing well: the worse off you are, the harder you try; the harder you try, the less likely you are to succeed. But once you're confident and sure of yourself, you become invincible.

Besides relaxation, you also need strength. In a modern Formula One car, the download is very strong. The car sometimes is as heavy as a big truck without power steering. All right, you can handle that so long as the car is going in the direction you want it to go; but the moment you have to make a quick or decisive correction, then you're going to have to call on all the strength you have. And if the car is misbehaving for 200-miles-plus and you have to make constant corrections, you're going to feel fagged out by the end of it. Stamina is a matter of strength. I'm lucky in that I get my second wind. I can be sweaty and tired and then all of a sudden I get that second wind and I can go on all day. It's the old high coming back into play.

I don't feel flattered when I'm complimented for some abstract quality like bravery, in that I go fast and I'm not frightened. If you were that imaginary passenger in my car, and you said, 'That was smooth; the braking, the turning; it all seemed part of a single move,' I would feel complimented.

To create that seamless drive is a matter of anticipation. I have to see the corner coming up and place my car in the right position to take it. For my imaginary passenger, the speed at which I approach it would seem tremendous; but if he went out week after week as I do, all that sensation of speed would be no more than hearing Muzak in a lift. It's not music, it's just background. The imaginary passenger might be scared: give him three weeks on his own in the car and he'd be saying, 'Can't you put a supercharger on this so it will go a bit faster?' If I come back to racing after a lay-off, it feels quick to me. As soon as I'm back in my stride, the car seems gutless.

Speed is nothing by itself. We go fastest down the long straights, but however fast you go down a straight, it's always a bit boring, especially if you're all alone on the straight. It's a bit more interesting if there are two or three other cars roaring down the straight along with you.

Slipstreaming them, sitting in their wake until they pull you forward, pulling out, trying to outbrake them: all that part of it is interesting. But not the speed. All those manoeuvres are interesting because they require care, and caution. Supposing there are two cars ahead of me down the straight and I decide to pull out and take on the leader: I have to take into account that the second man may pull out also. That's what you have to anticipate, for getting something wrong at that speed can be dicey. You are flat out on the accelerator and the track is only three cars wide: if there are several cars on one stretch of road on that straight, one of you is going to have to back off. Otherwise, speed alone is nothing. If you're like me, you're not conscious of it as speed; you're only conscious that you'd like to push the accelerator right through the floor.

Drivers don't question why they're racing. The top ones find it comes so normally that they believe anyone could do what they do. When it comes that easily, they feel guilty about it: that way lies underestimating the difficulties of the trade.

In fact, the analytical and the emotional aspects of driving are far closer together than A.J. admits. The choice between the two, or the combination employed, is a matter of emphasis rather than of a driver's psyche. No good driver can be unthinking; no successful driver can do without the competitiveness that led him into racing and its risks. Desire is as strong an emotion as any, and the top driver is a creature of his desires. That is, of his will.

Desire and envy play a part in moving any driver. If someone is on pole and I'm not, I feel both envy and desire: I envy him his position and I want to deprive him of the advantage he has gained. But, as with any aspect of driving, the first thing you must learn is your own limits; the second is the car's limits. You have to drive within those limits, and that requires discipline and will.

After a while in the trade, you know all the circuits, you've driven them, in races and practice and testing, countless times.

Thus you have fewer hesitations. The corners are a known factor. You have raised your blood pressure and your mental effort to take them many times before. What you have done before you should be able to do again. But there are always new problems, and there are always special corners that call on all a driver's intelligence and minimize his daredevil qualities. A lot of corners that feel good, because you go through them quickly, are in fact slow corners.

There is no such thing as the perfect lap. I never have done one and I never will. There is always something more to be squeezed out. If there are ten corners on a circuit, you may get nine of them perfectly, but will invariably get one of them less well than you might. All drivers are in search of an impossible perfect lap. But even an imperfect lap can give you pleasure. There is definitely such a thing as a beautiful-feeling corner.

When we used to have special qualifying tyres that were only good for two or three laps, I used to enjoy the pressures of that particular situation. I had two laps and at the end of that I had no tyres left and no second chance. In those circumstances, I couldn't miss a gear change, I couldn't allow myself to run wide on a corner, I couldn't brake too late. It all had to be done perfectly, and quickly. It was a perfect balance between going very, very quick and being very, very careful. An intriguing task.

You feel everything in the car. If you lock a wheel because you have braked too hard or too late, your steering goes: you feel that. The tyres are locked in place and it feels like you're sliding on ice. You have to release your brake to get your steering back.

I always belt myself in very tightly: so tightly that the mechanics usually get red-faced strapping me into the car. But with two straps across your shoulders, two across your hips and two round your crotch, if the car moves so much as a quarter of an inch, you're immediately aware of it. I must not think: 'Was that my bum moving, or was it the car?' I like instant feedback.

But all sorts of forces are moving around you all the time. If you brake too hard, the front of your car dips and that doesn't help; the back will get too light and slide out. If you get your braking at exactly the right point on the corner, if you select the right gear, get the car at its right height and then accelerate through as smoothly as possible, you will get the best possible exit speed.

I keep my eyes straight ahead of me. The right spot to catch the apex of the curve is like a clear white spot that grows bigger and bigger and more visible as you get into your rhythm. After a while, you will always clip the same apex lap after lap. As you accelerate out, you have to avoid having the back come out on you. If that happens, the tyres are going sideways instead of forward and you're scrubbing speed. My old man was big on that lesson: tyres are designed to go forwards, not sideways.

Going through the corner, though, you feel everything in the car. It's completely connected to you and you feel every twitch. Your bum transmits the information to your brain. Thinking is not required, or possible. It's all too quick. If you made even a very rapid series of calculations, by the time you'd completed them, you'd be in the fence. So that most driving around corners is a matter of reflex and experience.

The need for experience is one of the reasons it is almost impossible to make it successfully in Formula One as a beginner. You can't make corrections until you've lived through your mistakes.

It is reflex that takes my foot off the brake if I'm going into a corner and my brakes lock up. But a normal reflex is exactly the opposite: a beginning driver would tend to push harder on the brake hoping that his brake will slow him down. The net result of that reflex is to plough into the armco. And much of what you have to do in racing is contrary to one's normal instincts. When you are heading into a wall at 130 m.p.h., it is against instinct to take your foot off the brake. So you have to teach yourself to do it naturally, so that it becomes a reflex.

There are two particularly anxious situations in racing. The first is when you have a comfortable lead and everything is going well. You're near the end of the race and suddenly someone comes up behind to challenge you. 'The bastard!' you think, 'he's trying to take my grand prix away from me!' The other is when you're catching up someone very slowly, gaining a second

135

every lap. There you are, ten laps from the end, ten seconds behind, and you think: 'I can catch up all right, but will I be able to pass him?'

I mention both those situations because in almost every circumstance you depend not just on yourself, but on your car. True, the car always has a little more to give, but do you? Subconsciously, when the reserve is needed from inside yourself, you can usually come up with it. You can always get an extra half-second out of yourself. The car obeys you, so it is you who have to find that extra half-second in yourself. I can think of many times that I have gone out and done quickish laps and thought: 'I can't get anything more out of this.' Then at the end of the day it will turn out I got a second or more out of it. Part lies in the preparation of the car, but the rest is getting into your groove and pushing yourself beyond what you think are your own limits.

Going into corners, drivers face something called a 'confidence lift', which is really a lack-of-confidence lift. A driver takes his foot off the accelerator for a fraction of a second: he's not sure he can actually take the corner at a higher speed.

You have to attune yourself to keeping your foot on the floor as much as possible. Lifting off means losing time. Speed is not an abstract entity; a driver doesn't see the world rushing by him; it is a question of habituation. Wherever you are, at the end of every straight there is a corner. You see it coming up. You see those lovely signs reading 5, 4, 3, 2, 1 and it becomes a game. I might start off braking at the 200 mark, then at the 150 mark, and all the time I'll be saying to myself, 'Come on, A.J., you can do better than that.' Bit by bit I talk myself into braking later and later.

Until the inevitable moment when I've gone in so quickly it has affected my exit from the corner; the wheels have locked, I've gone wide and messed up the exit. The next time around, I try to find the optimum mark: that point at which, going in quickest, I can also come out quickest. And sometimes it pays to have a little bit of a lift, to set the attitude of your car right, to get a cleaner exit. What's the use of going in like a rocket if you come out like a snail? Slow in, fast out, is much better than fast in, slow out.

With a season that encompasses Argentina and Brazil in mid-summer, the South African Rand, Europe from spring through the summer and the United States and Canada in the early autumn, drivers also face a bewildering variety of climates, altitudes and track conditions. They have roasted in Buenos Aires and Rio and frozen, regularly, in Montreal, seen sleet at the Nürburgring and been drenched at Zolder, but whatever the extremities, they have had to drive in them.

No experienced driver minds a damp, slippery track; if anything, that adds a bit to the excitement of the race. Rain is something else. No one likes the rain, though there are some drivers who are supposedly better in the rain than others. The worst part of the track in the rain is the straight. You literally see nothing. Most people will not believe it when I say 'nothing', but I mean nothing. You take your foot off and drive by the side of the track or in what you hope is the general direction. The danger lies not in your skidding – at least not on the straight – but in your inability to anticipate: if something happens ahead of you and there is a car on the track, you will literally plough into him before you even see him.

There are, of course, drivers like Vittorio Brambilla, or Hans Stuck when he was still driving in Formula One, who seem to add speed in the rain: as though it were their one hope of registering a result. Speeds do fall off in rain: by perhaps five per cent. So that speeds of well over 150 m.p.h. will still be registered, while driving blind.

Anyone who sits behind a pack of cars in the rain, foot in, is a bloody maniac, but there are some around. The danger is more than doubled, and the wise driver takes all possible precautions. Most drivers know how to handle a slippery track, being familiar with skidding even when the track is dry – on oil, or dust, or just by hard cornering; the solution is simply to drive with much greater care and smoothness. It is the sudden movement

137

that puts you into trouble, and emergencies which are dangerous. I won my first grand prix in Austria on a greasy track and
I don't really mind the wet.

Nonetheless, conditions for the driver in the wet are far from
ideal! He drives for two hours literally soaked through to the
skin, bathed in the rooster tails that come up from the cars in
front and land in his cockpit; his visor fogs up and he keeps
trying to wipe it clear. It would be a lot easier if regulations
were enforced to put some sort of rain-guard behind the wheels
to prevent spray.

The truth is, however, that you get used to driving in all
conditions: rain, great heat, wind, dirty tracks. I've seen young
drivers being lifted out of their cockpits at the end of a race,
utterly exhausted with heat prostration. Or I've noted during
the race how their necks start swaying from side to side because
the muscles aren't strong enough to support the weight of their
heads under the G-forces they have to face. In time, the muscles
build up. I can face any race that's run in a clockwise direction,
but at Interlagos in Brazil, we race counter-clockwise and my
neck hurts appallingly. It's all a matter of building up specialized muscle. Your ankles, for instance, get very strong from the
constant to-and-fro with the accelerator and brake. Driving gets
easier as you put in the years, and the heat never really did
bother me; I seem to get up to some inner temperature of my
own and just stay there. It's like getting a second wind. Still,
the average driver will lose something like five or six pounds in
a race.

The G-forces are the greatest contributors to fatigue. Sometimes they are strong enough to make me hold my breath. When
I go through some corners I find it hard to do two things at once:
breathe normally and steer. I feel the forces like a great weight
on my chest and as though someone were leaning hard on my
head, which feels twice its weight. The braking, too, is heavy
on those forces, though you feel it less thanks to being strapped
in so tightly; and the kick of the acceleration can seem to push
you right back through your seat.

On the whole, these are minor discomforts which you forget
in the heat of the race. The mind takes over from the body and
makes you forget its state of unease. Most of us take our racing

very personally and that buries all the problems we face somewhere deep in the subconscious, so that you're not aware of
them until after the race.

I don't race, of course, against any specific individual; I race
against all of them, as individuals. The mental tension is much
harder than the physical, especially if I make a mistake. I
literally seethe with anger if I'm not first or quickest. But mistakes have their compensations. It is good to make a mistake
now and again, for all of us are written down for one or two
frights a year. I like to get them over early and make sure
they're frights and nothing more. The mind takes care of them.
It concentrates on its target, which is to get to the front, and
therefore past anybody who's ahead of you. If you have to pass
seven people to get to the front, that's the task. As long as there
is another car or another driver ahead of you, you have to beat
him. But they become just objects to get past. So are you to
another driver. Not a person but an object. Hence the mistakes.

'Mistakes'. Some of which are fatal.

*A driver's professional life-span is short enough anyway. After
it is finished, he is just a former racing driver and has to find
some other justification for his existence, a task which many have
found difficult. Few of the former greats survive; the fatality-rate
is high. Jean Manuel Fangio, probably the greatest of them all,
is still seen at the circuits occasionally, impersonating a memory.*

*In alphabetical order, the honoured dead include: Alberto As-
cari, killed practising in a friend's car; Lorenzo Bandini, who
died racing; Jean Behra in a non-Formula One race; Felice
Bonetto, racing in Mexico; Jo Bonnier at Le Mans; Eugenio
Castellotti, testing; Jim Clark in a Formula Two race; Peter
Collins at the Nürburgring and Piers Courage at Zandvoort;
Patrick Depailler at Hockenheim, testing after a long night drive;
Luigi Fagioli during practice at Monaco; Giuseppe Farina in a
car crash, and Mike Hawthorn likewise; Bruce McLaren in testing; Luigi Musso during the French Grand Prix and Ronnie
Peterson during the Italian; Peter Revson in South Africa during
pre-race testing; Jochen Rindt in Italy, and two Rodriguez, one
brother in Germany, the other in Mexico; Harry Schell in Eng-*

land; Jo Siffert and Wolfgang von Trips, taking spectators with him.

And many others.

The first requirement is making it; the second, surviving it; and for the survivors, using it. As it happens, the more experienced and the more successful suffer a higher proportion of fatalities. A.J. says they're the ones who are trying the hardest. By the same token, they are also the ones with the clearest knowledge of the risks and how to minimize them. Yet those who put it on the line most often run the greatest risk of coming unstuck.

You don't get to the top of this profession, or any profession, by mistake. It's too competitive and too political for someone to arse it in. You can arse one grand prix but you can't win consistently just on luck. You get on top by continually going harder, mentally or physically, than your competitors. Just trying that little bit harder or driving that little bit better. Hence the chance of coming unstuck. If I take a 130 m.p.h. corner at 130 m.p.h. I'm much more likely to come unstuck than the driver taking it at 125 or 128.

I think it fair to say that we're a callous lot about death. If I were killed tomorrow, Frank would probably say, 'That's too bad; A.J. was a bit of a character.' The truth may not be attractive, but it remains true. Frank is in the business of motor racing and in his plans, I am a cog. If I go, Frank must replace me. If Carlos were killed, I'd say, 'Poor Carlos'; and then I'd ask Frank who he had in mind to take his place.

It's something we have to live with. All of us. It sounds cold, but it's just one of the many sad facts of the business I happen to be in. We are bloody mercenaries and we can't get hysterical every time someone gets killed. If you wept over each death during a civil war in the Congo you'd have no business being a mercenary. It wouldn't work in the Congo; it won't work on the circuit.

In the old days, teams withdrew from the sport, drivers gave up their careers in sorrow at the loss of a friend. It was a form of respect.

140

Racing was very different back then. It was neither so practical nor so professional and there weren't as many interests involved. Who can afford to stop now? Would the sponsors approve? The circuit owners? The constructors? Those were amateur days, even as to death. We've changed our attitudes, having seen more of death than they had, and seen it clearly; watched it on the box. Who mourns anyone today? Who wears little bits of black cloth in their lapels? What widows get themselves kitted out in black?

When Ascari was killed and Lancia withdrew their cars, it was against a backdrop of a public who reacted to death, sudden, violent death, very differently from the way we see it. The papers and the box are full of death. Thousands and thousands get killed on the roads every year. Almost everyone who drives has seen the blood and the wreckage. Back then, if Lancia had gone on racing, the public would have thought they were a callous lot and not bought their cars.

Today all is commerce and cold blood. Do I approve or disapprove? I don't do either. I recognize things the way they are. Alfa didn't pull out when Patrick was killed. They got on with racing, which was why Depailler was testing and why they built the car for him to test.

If I got killed, I wouldn't expect Frank to pull out, and I don't think Frank would even dream that I wanted him to. We all know what we're doing, we all know the risks and we've all got our money and our deals as a form of compensation. My deal is that I get so many pounds to drive for Frank and do the best I can: risks included, because the risks are necessary to get the results. If I get killed in the course of duty, that's my bad luck. It shouldn't be anyone else's bad luck.

But if I'm going to kill myself in a car, it had better be worth it. People call up all the time and say, 'Look, drive this, drive that.' And I say, 'Sure, give me X thousand pounds and I'll drive it.' They wet their pants. They say, 'But the car didn't even cost that much!' I tell them it doesn't matter how much the car cost, they can always make another one. But my life comes dear. Divide my total earnings in Formula One by the number of races I do for Frank each year and that's my price for putting myself on the line. If I hurt myself driving for less, I'd lose my

141

money from Formula One. It's a cash transaction. Even death is.

Obviously, I think about the risk. All drivers do, whatever they may say to the contrary. But I weigh it all up. For X pounds, I do sixteen races, and I won't do even one more for less than that amount. Every race I do is a calculated risk. But once I get in the car, I've committed myself and the risk no longer plays a part. Analysis stops when the car heads out of the pit-lane.

It remains true that motor-racing, alongside bull-fighting, boxing and, very rarely, horse-racing, is one of those rare sports where an athlete risks his life. In any other sport, the prospect of a fatal accident is unlikely; in motor-racing that accident is a clear consequence of the sport itself. The statistics are far too regular to suggest otherwise: an accident every five grands prix for most drivers, or two or three a year of what A.J. calls 'frights'. And one of those, as Gilles Villeneuve once pointed out with great sangfroid, is almost bound to be a 'big one', involving physical damage of some sort.

To get past the fear barrier, to deny the risk, the sort of clinical mania that A.J. has described is necessary. Saints wanted to get to God regardless. The personal consequences did not come into it. They would fast for forty days until they spun off and saw God. It was self-induced blindness.

You've made your bed, you learn how to lie in it. My best friend, Brian Maguire, with whom I lived when I came to London, got killed at Brands Hatch in an Aurora race. I didn't look on that as Brian getting killed motor-racing; it was just Brian getting killed. It would have been the same if someone had called up and said Brian had been run over by a truck or got himself electrocuted. The fact was that Brian was dead. I was upset by his death, but not by the way he was killed.

Carlos Pace, who used to drive for Brabham, was killed in a plane crash, like Graham Hill and Tony Brise. He was a very professional driver and I felt sorry for him: but neither more nor less than if he'd been killed in his cockpit during a race. The fact of his death comes first.

Most drivers, myself included, work on the principle that it will never happen to them. And I think it won't happen to me. If I didn't work on that principle, I don't see how I could be doing it. And when something does happen and someone is killed, what's the good of sitting there in a heap and moaning, 'Aaargh! that could have happened to me.' When you start doing that, that's the time to give up.

Every driver I've ever talked to has his own methodology for disarming death. Niki Lauda once said after his accident that he had come to a point, after driving as long as he had, when he no longer thought about the risk of death, because it had become a familiar; it sat alongside him all the time and became a face he knew and accepted as much as he accepted himself. Ronnie Peterson, killed at Monza, said that he rigorously excluded any thought of death from his mind. He said death was irrelevant. When it happened, it happened: much worse was to suffer pain or mutilation or paralysis. Gunnar Nilsson, who died of cancer, said he would far rather have died quickly, in a car.

Sometimes, however, it would seem as though death were as attractive to drivers as life. Death becomes for these just another competitor to outwit. Others have taken a philosophical view; they were born to die, and what was the fuss all about? One who came closest to meeting death on its own ground was Patrick Depailler, whose day of reckoning came at Hockenheim in 1980; Patrick said that he never expected to 'retire' from racing. The idea had no appeal for him.

Perhaps drivers can face their own deaths with that sort of detachment. Perception, too, hardens. The soul thickens, it forms a carapace. One of the secrets in this process is that most drivers think of death as a 'mistake'. It shouldn't have happened, but did.

Fatal accidents often come from mistakes; and as often from trying that little bit too hard. Worse still is when the big one comes, not from a mistake of your own, but from someone else's mistake. It wasn't Ronnie's mistake that killed him at Monza. It was one of those split-second pieces of dreadful luck. Something needn't have happened, but it did. And every one of us

143

can relate how one mechanical component of the car or another has failed. We all know that something may break at a critical moment. I'd be telling a lie if I said the possibility didn't enter my mind.

Drivers are very conscious beings. But the subconscious still plays its part. To go through a corner fast, really fast, a driver has to prepare his subconscious; yet the preparation of that subconscious is a conscious act. He goes through the corner, he lifts off a bit; he thinks, 'I could go through that a little faster.' The next lap, he does exactly the same thing – he lifts off again. 'Why?' he asks himself. Slowly, lap by lap, he brings himself to go through that corner as fast as he can. Once he's done that, he's pushed through the subconscious fear and he can do it lap after lap without thinking.

That doesn't mean the fear is not always within us. It shows in all sorts of ways. Going through a corner flat out, you know you'd be more comfortable lifting off. You can feel how much easier it would be. But, despite the fear, your mind tells you that you *can* go through that corner flat, because you've done so in the past. Yet you have to talk yourself into doing what you know you can do. That's a by-product of fear. Like a kid sitting on a high wall and thinking how far away the ground looks. There comes the point when he finally makes up his mind and jumps. But not until after he's had a fight with himself. For us, that fight is a daily occurrence.

The trade is full of scary moments. As when you think you might be losing control, the car slewing sideways through a corner. Nine times out of ten, though the fear hits you, you don't have enough time for it to register properly: you correct the slide. Or you don't. The competition can scare you: someone pulls out of the slipstream just as you're about to. It's only afterwards that you think just how dicey that could have been. But I don't dwell on the scares. If you give them time to grow inside you, they become more important than they really are. The end result of that is, you go slow.

Drivers don't like to think on those moments of fear. If they did, they wouldn't be driving. Some people think the world divides into people who think and people who act, but there are many people who do both, and I'm one of them. In my car, I

144

condition myself not to think. Thus I can go through a big shunt and still come back, not even thinking about the fear or the might-have-been. For all of us there are thoughts which we refuse.

Much of it is conditioned reflex. Almost nothing that can happen in a car is happening to you for the first time. When crises arise, you are internally prepared for them and your system tells you how to cope. I can concentrate 1000 per cent and be in total control and a crisis will come up; I don't push through or below a certain level in my mind, because I've accustomed myself not to. I operate within my own capacities. It's the old safety valve at work again. I can block almost anything out of my mind.

I do that same sort of blocking out about the sport in general. When Patrick was killed at Hockenheim in 1980, I could imagine what had happened. He'd had a long drive, he had breakfast, he went out and put out. The next thing, he was dead. Poor old Patrick. If I asked myself too many questions about it, I'd just be waking up the fear in myself, and I can neither afford to do that nor allow it to happen.

Drivers sometimes joke about death and people might think we are cold bastards. Patrick bought it last week. What does that mean? He bought it. We know what it means. We seem callous, but it's our way of glossing over the fact; it's how we reject his death. Or our own.

Neither Patrick nor any other driver I've known who is now dead sits with me. They are not ghosts. Nor are they forgotten. But when I went to Hockenheim after Patrick's death, I had a good look at the corner where he crashed. I analyzed it. I might be coming up against the same corner and I wanted to know where and how he lost it. And I decided if they didn't put some catch-fencing up there, I wasn't racing. At least we try to learn from what went wrong for another driver.

Yet there are times when you think you've lost it and you know you're heading for one of the big ones; you're completely in the lap of the gods, and then by a stroke of luck you'll come back on the circuit, you'll gather it all up. Reporters come up and say that that was the best piece of driving they've ever seen. Modestly, you admit you calculated the whole thing.

145

At other times you are facing an accident and you've done wonders to position your car so that when it hits it won't hurt you, and no one appreciates your skill: just because you've had an accident. Making sure you're not hurt, or hurt less than you might be, requires a lot of skill. I can be not only pleased at being spared, but also quite proud of having made the right decision fast enough.

Backwards is the best way to hit anything. The impact is absorbed through the gearbox, the back suspension and the engine before it gets to the driver. Nine times out of ten you hit sideways, because you are fighting the potential shunt all the way. Forwards is the worst.

It's only right that death in racing should be talked about: if only because a number of deaths could be avoided – by stronger cars, safer circuits, quicker medical attention, better marshalling. The cars do get safer and safer, but death is part of our job and you can't pretend it does not exist.

As a driver, I know that if you don't take the 'it can't happen to me' road, there are not that many other roads you can take and sit quietly in your car. When you think it can happen to you, that is the time to pack up your gear and head back to the farm.

That moment comes to every racer. The thought of retirement grows on him, little by little. He finds himself thinking about it more and more. It seems ever more desirable. He sleeps a little less after each race. He enjoys driving a little less. His edge goes off, his appetite diminishes. At the end of that stage, all he wants after practice or racing is to get out of the car. Then he says to himself, 'I've survived another day, here I am.' Courage comes when a driver recognizes that moment and quits.

Many drivers reach that point but can't give up, or won't. It could be that they still want to prove a point, that they're better than they're given credit for. It may be that a racer hasn't settled everything in his mind that he wants to. Or perhaps he hasn't got the financial security yet that he is striving for. But if I felt that and I had to give up racing tomorrow, I'm all right. I'm all right financially, that's the main thing. And I've got my reputation, I've made it. I don't have to prove myself.

But then you read in the papers a great big story about a film stunt man who won the Monte Carlo rally, and way in the back of the paper there's a little paragraph saying that Emerson Fittipaldi, twice World Champion, is retiring from motor racing. That's all. Quick oblivion. Which is unpleasant. Anyone who did what Emerson did deserves better.

Well, before Emerson finally quit, he was going through a long bad patch. A lot of people said Emerson had lost his balls, Emerson was sparing himself, he was thinking about his kiddies back home and he wasn't driving that hard.

That may even be true, but I wonder if it wasn't totally unconscious. Before he quit, did he will himself to go slower, or did he think he was still going as fast as ever? Do you reach a point where your eight-tenths drive seems to you a lot more than that? A point where, though you're driving as fast as you know, it's nothing compared to what it was a few years before? I don't think you'd ever know that. You could always blame it on the car or on some other factor. But the sad truth is, you'd be braking a little earlier and putting the power on just a little bit later.

This easing up has become commonplace. The last multiple champions, apart from Niki Lauda, were Jackie Stewart and Emerson Fittipaldi. James Hunt won it and went into a decline through a useless car and, if A.J. is right, because his heart was no longer in it. Mario Andretti won it once, and in the succeeding years could not come close to matching his 1978 performance. Jody Scheckter won it, and after one rich season with Ferrari with appalling results, retired.

A lot of people say, now I'm World Champion, I won't try so hard. But I am not racing to be World Champion, which I am and which can't be gainsaid. I go racing because I still want to, and because I want people to respect me for that. I have to be quickest for me, not for anyone else. That attitude has helped me brush aside the pressure and the politics. What gets my blood up is to be in the car, racing. I know it's insular and narrow-minded, but it works for me.

I don't know how long I can keep that competitive spirit going. No one can foresee that, because it's a state of mind. I might wake up one morning, a lovely spring morning on my farm and think, 'There's no way I'm going to leave this behind me.' My appetite might have waned, or business might be good and I might be deriving equal pleasure from that.

To repeat:

At the moment, I'm still single-minded. I've only got attention to spare for what I'm actually doing. God willing, if I get through it all, I'll be a bit broader in my mind than I am now. I know it is going on, because I seem to change all the time. My tastes change, and I expect that the day will come when I know who I am and I will settle for that. Today, it's all change and movement. Daily, I find myself more relaxed, more philosophical.

Of course I'm going to try to be Champion again. What else, or what more can I do? I have faith in my team and I know I'm good. That being so, my chances have to be as good as anyone else's.

But somewhere deep down inside me, I recognize that I'm very cold-blooded. I may be sentimental or nostalgic; I like to think of myself in another period like the thirties or forties where there were fewer restrictions on life and life was freer and gayer, but I am a cold person. Very cold. Indifferent and cold.

Beverly would agree I'm cold and unromantic. I love her very much and treasure my family life; I plan to be no less than a patriarch with kids and property. But few things actually touch me. I am not moved. I do not shed many tears. I feel for the underdog, it is possible for me to cry over injustice, but death leaves me cold. Yet if my child were killed, I'd break into a million pieces. Three years ago, before we had Christian, I wouldn't have believed it. Now that I've got him and experience the joy of him, I could not imagine life without him. So a lot is changing.

A lot of my life has been repression. I check myself a lot. In feeling, certainly. I was a kid who went dancing and wouldn't ask the girl to dance in case she rejected me. Pride is involved, and insecurity. Stubbornness and an inability to take things as they come, or to let my true feelings show.

As I said, I'm an egotist's son and an egotist myself. My egotistical high comes from the actual racing, not from its side-shows. Maybe when I retire, I'll let myself go. Or perhaps I am frightened at the idea of letting myself go.

Meanwhile, the repression remains strong. I have to sit on myself. I may fancy a disco or a girl or a few beers but I have to say to myself all the time, 'No you can't, no you won't; it's salad and bed-time for you.' The more you repress, the bigger the build-up and the eventual explosion. Every Sunday after a race I'm like a balloon that's been pricked with a pin – the air just whistles out of me. Then comes the big meal and the laughs. And there are going to be a lot more of those, because one day there's not going to be another Sunday morning after the last Sunday night.

I have to sit on myself because I know what I want and where I'm going in life. My biggest want is to be on top, and that means sitting on the beast in me to get there.

If I live through this, I may become a great bore, but I am going to enjoy having lived through it. I'll have worked for it, I'll have survived the dice and I'll deserve a good remainder to my life.

Meanwhile, I think a great deal more than I say. There are people who can say exactly what they think, in speech or in writing. They can express the whole complexity of their life. In my case, whether through laziness or concealment, I can only express a small part of it. Perhaps I have neither the time nor the desire to put myself into words.

So far, I have expressed my life in my racing, and who I am will not come out until I've finished.

Mombasa, 26.1.81–
Boston, 11.3.81

Championship Diary 1980

1979 had been a good season for A.J. and the Williams team, with A.J. dominating the second half of the season in spectacular fashion. In many ways, 1979 was the year in which the sport began to take notice of A.J. – not merely because he began winning, but because he was beginning to show the kinds of maturity that mark the potential champion: the ability to drive well within the limits of a car, the technique of finishing races and finishing them consistently, a kind of higher seriousness about the professional tasks before him and a rise to the peak of physical and psychological performance.

A season, especially a championship season, is like a carefully constructed edifice. It is put together brick by brick. It is not a spectacular display that's good only for the day, like some monstrous ice-cream that will melt away in the consuming. In a championship season, all results count, and must be made to count. Consistency is the single most important factor: the bricks must be made to hold together and one result must build on another. A good car must be perfected and adapted to each circuit, and here simplicity is the watchword, for the simple car is the most flexible and adaptable.

It also requires great concentration from all the members of the team. The team manager or boss must keep all the balls in the air at all times; the designer must find those solutions which are not simply makeshifts but will last throughout sixteen races; mechanics can make no mistakes; drivers must work together as a team and have regard for each other's and the team's interests.

As Charlie Crichton-Stuart said earlier, the 1980 season and the title did not just fall into A.J.'s lap: he had to work for it, race after race, through disappointment, triumph, controversy and, in the closing stages, a fierce challenge from the young

151

Nelson Piquet. What follows is how A.J. saw the season, from its beginning in Argentina in late January, to its triumphant conclusion — in Montreal, where he won the title; at Watkins Glen, where he showed that he had every intention, as champion, of remaining strictly competitive; and in Australia, where he made his triumphant homecoming.

We were all conscious that we had been a little late in bringing out the 07 car in 1979, which had made us more than a little unreliable, as any new car takes some time getting sorted out. But when the 07 had made its appearance and been thoroughly refined, it became clear to all of us that we had a very superior car. It was reliable, adaptable, simple and quick, and all those things in greater measure than any other car in Formula One. On the other hand, during the winter, we knew, many other constructors would have worked no less hard than we, and I personally was far from being sure that the superiority we had shown at the end of the 1979 season would still be ours in 1980. And I was right. You can't stand still in this game: sooner or later, everyone catches up with you.

To make sure we weren't caught unprepared, we decided to go down to Argentina in December and do three or four days' testing. And though this is a costly exercise — there is nothing cheap about sending a car, a driver, spares and mechanics six thousand miles by air — it more than proved its value. We were able to dial the car into the circuit and do some very profitable work with Goodyear, who provided our tyres, and thus, when January and the race came along, we could just roll the car out of the trailer and assert our superiority over the rest of the field: I not only took pole position, but won the race, though not without the usual arguments along the way.

For, towards the end of practice, the Buenos Aires circuit, a huge, flat track laid out in the suburbs of the city, was beginning to break up in alarming fashion. So bad was the track that a drivers' meeting was called to determine whether or not we would race at all. Fortunately, the majority of drivers, myself included, proved to be in favour of racing: we had all come a long way to race, the spectators had paid their money, everyone was present and accounted for, and we thought we ought to get on with it and not just pack our bags and go home. After all, if the track was bad, it was equally bad for all.

My team-mate, Carlos Reutemann, was on his home track, and the idol of the crowds, and the Williams victory in Argentina provided just the sort of lift the team needed to put it into gear for 1980. It set our level and served notice on all the other teams that we considered 1980 *our* year. All we had to do was keep ourselves at the same pitch for the rest of the year.

Argentine Grand Prix/Buenos Aires/13 January/53 laps, 316.314 km.
Grid: JONES, Laffite, Pironi, Piquet, De Angelis, Andretti, Patrese, Villeneuve, Jabouille, Reutemann.
Results: JONES, Piquet, Rosberg, Daly, Giacomelli, Prost.
Points: JONES, 9; Piquet, 6; Rosberg, 4; Daly, 3; Giacomelli, 2; Prost, 1.

Brazil, there is ready agreement, was one of A.J.'s poorest ever races. The cause? Distraction probably; or over-confidence; or possibly a distaste for the ugly sprawl of São Paulo.

In terms of layout, Interlagos is one of the finest circuits there is, yet it is far from being my favourite track. Getting there through city traffic is hell and, once you're there, the organization leaves something to be desired, which is a polite way of saying it's chaotic.

But that's not all. It is also fiercely punishing physically, and for a reason even most people who follow the sport would not know about: that Interlagos is one of the very few circuits around the world laid out counter-clockwise, and this makes it very, very hard on the neck. There are a lot of fast corners, all in this unusual anti-clockwise direction and, after about fifteen minutes out on the track, you become acutely conscious of this. It is the only circuit, for instance, at which I need a masseur in attendance; if he weren't there to attack me for twenty minutes after each session, my neck would literally stiffen up completely and I'd be useless. The neck muscles, hugely built up to race clockwise, are simply not up to the strain.

I qualified on the fifth row, drove the race without inspiration and, though I finished third – which wasn't bad, as it gave me

153

13 points from the two South American races – it is not a race I am proud of. To this day, Frank calls it the Mobil Economy Run, because, where I'm usually lucky to finish with two or three pints of fuel, that day I finished with no less that four gallons in the tanks!

Brazilian Grand Prix/Interlagos/27 January/40 laps, 318.4 km.
Grid: Jabouille, Pironi, Villeneuve, Reutemann, Laffite, Arnoux, De Angelis, Scheckter, Piquet, JONES.
Results: Arnoux, De Angelis, JONES, Pironi, Prost, Patrese.
Points: JONES, 13; Arnoux, 9; Piquet, De Angelis, 6; Rosberg 4.

South Africa and Kyalami, with its thatched hut ranch and insufferably slow service, its icy pool in which only the bravest swim, its tennis courts where the Formula One family play, is high on everyone's list of favourite circuits. Being over 5000 feet up, however, it strongly favours turbo-powered engines. As A.J. relates:

I like South Africa. It's a good place to relax, play tennis and, at last, order your meals in English! The circuit is interesting, challenging and fast. The secret is to get the car going as fast as you can down the long straight, and I can remember the days when you had to get your car set up just right to take the approach corner, Barbecue, flat out: it's easier now.

I qualified eighth, got a tremendous start, was actually leading the two Renault turbos down the straight as far as the bridge, and then they passed me. I was third. Laffite passed me. I was fourth, with Carlos fifth. Thirty laps into the race, my gearbox bearings gave way and that was that.

I was not in the best of moods, disappointed at not finishing and wanting to get off the track fast. But Frank said, 'No, I want you to go down to the Leyland hospitality tent.' 'All right,' I said, this being part of what I'm paid to do. So I went down to their marquee and had a few beers with the top people at Leyland, minding my own business, when this chap came up to me, pissed out of his brains, and told me to piss off. Slightly obstreperously. In fact, finally he took a lunge at me. Well, not being in the most pacific of moods, I whacked him a couple of times and he hit the deck. It turned out later he was the Leyland distributor in Praetoria, which is why I don't expect any big discounts up there! It worked out all right in the end, though; the next day the local papers carried a headline saying DRUNK ATTACKS SPORTSMAN IN HOSPITALITY TENT. It wasn't quite that way, but it saved us all embarrassment.

South African Grand Prix/Kyalami/1 March/78 laps, 320.112 km.
Grid: Jabouille, Arnoux, Piquet, Laffite, Pironi, Reutemann, Depailler, JONES, Scheckter, Villeneuve.
Results: Arnoux, Laffite, Pironi, Piquet, Reutemann, Mass.
Points: Arnoux, 18; JONES, 13; Piquet, 9; Pironi, 7, De Angelis, Laffite, 6.

The US Grand Prix West at Long Beach is a race I have always liked: liked well enough to have bought a house (since sold) within easy reach of the city and its picturesque street race. I like the friendliness, the openness and the effort the locals put into making their race a success.

But it will remain for me a race marred by the serious accident which paralysed my old friend and team-mate Clay Regazzoni. For some reason, too, neither my car nor Carlos's seemed properly set up for Long Beach, and Nelson Piquet was obviously going to be the man to watch; he was on pole and a second and a half faster than I. I had qualified fifth and Carlos seventh.

It was a race also marked by numerous retirements and accidents. Some ten laps in, I was lying third, with Piquet in front and Depailler behind him. After a prolonged duel, I managed to overtake Patrick, but I seemed unable to do anything to catch up with Nelson, and two-thirds of the way through the race whilst lapping Giacomelli, he went into the side of my car and put me out of the race. It was after this race that I began to sense the threat posed to us by Nelson Piquet, who now led the championship alongside Arnoux.

US Grand Prix West/Long Beach/ 30 March/80 laps, 260 km.
Grid: Piquet, Arnoux, Depailler, Lammers, JONES, Giacomelli, Reutemann, Patrese, Pironi, Villeneuve.
Results: Piquet, Patrese, Fittipaldi, Watson, Scheckter, Pironi.
Points: Arnoux, Piquet, 18; JONES, 13; Pironi, 8; Patrese, 7; De Angelis, Laffite, 6.

155

The two seasons, the European and the non-European, differ radically in their tone. The European season has tradition behind it. Tradition means, all too often, just a lot of dead weight: inadequate circuits, groupies, parasites and hangers-on, all the surface people who want to be seen; the non-European races are more exotic, livelier and, for that reason, probably more experimental. Europe is for business and, for most drivers, as for A.J., it is home.

The European season is my favourite time of the year. It is just more organized, and easier on everybody. There aren't those long flights; you get to the track on a Thursday and you have some chance of getting home by Sunday night; you get a rhythm going in your life and feel you have a base of sorts. I'm one of those people who always feels better if I know where I'm going to be when.

After South Africa, we did a lot of testing for Goodyear. In fact, during the season, we tested at nearly every circuit, sometimes months before its grand prix. And, as we tested for Goodyear, we were able to sort our car out, too. All of it was a help.

Zolder, in Belgium, is on everyone's list of disliked circuits. Sandy, wet, inhospitable, it is many miles away from civilization. At the time of the Belgian Grand Prix, the great battle between the warring authorities of FISA and the constructors' organization, FOCA, was already foreshadowed. Everyone's mood was sour, and few will forget the belligerent press conference Balestre held on race day: the sport would bend to his will, he implied, or he would force it to do so.

Though we were all watching the quarrel looming, my mind was only on the race and getting a result after the failure in South Africa. During qualifying, however, I seemed to be unable to do much better than third or fourth in my race-car, and finally, not far from the end, it simply broke down. I raced back to the pits to get into the spare car, only to find that Carlos was out in it. I admit to being pissed off at this, but Frank waited until Carlos had made the best use of his fresh tyres; then he

156

put on another new set for me, put five gallons into the tank and off I went: to pole position! Satisfying, that!

But we had had serious problems with understeering throughout practice, and Pironi had been just behind us all through qualifying; when it came to the race, he got a superb start and walked away with it. I had to content myself with second place and ever-increasing understeer. As Carlos took third, the result was good for Williams, and I have no complaints about the six points I picked up for myself.

Belgian Grand Prix/Zolder/4 May/72 laps, 306.864 km.
Grid: JONES, Pironi, Laffite, Reutemann, Jabouille, Arnoux, Piquet, De Angelis, Jarier, Depailler.
Results: Pironi, JONES, Reutemann, Arnoux, Jarier, Villeneuve.
Points: Arnoux, 21; JONES, 19; Piquet, 18; Pironi, 17; Patrese, 7; De Angelis, Laffite, Reutemann, 6.

The Monaco Grand Prix is one I cannot stand. It's not just the poseurs and their yachts, though they're bad enough; it's not just the aggro getting to and from the pits to do my job; it's the race itself, which is just a bloody procession. The truth is that the cars have outgrown the circuit, which is too narrow for anyone to have a chance of overtaking without taking a hefty gamble. It's also exceedingly boring to drive. Boring and frustrating, and though, for its prestige, I'd dearly love to win it, I'm not alone in thinking it were better it died a natural death.

I qualified third, made a bloody good start and got into second place as I went up the hill, missing the shambles taking place behind me. I was surprised how slowly Pironi was going, and how he was holding me up, for I had the legs of him and was sitting there just waiting for him to make a mistake. Unfortunately for me, before he had a chance to make one, my own gearbox blew up and I had to coast into the pits. It was another disappointment, because I felt certain I could have won that race. Nor was that my only disappointment. By then I was beginning to realize how much every single point was likely to mean to me, and I hadn't managed to score at all.

Monaco Grand Prix/Monte Carlo/18 May/76 laps, 251.712 km.
Grid: Pironi, Reutemann, JONES, Piquet, Laffite, Villeneuve, Depailler, Giacomelli, Jarier, Prost.

Results: Reutemann, Laffite, Piquet, Mass, Villeneuve, Fittipaldi.
Points: Piquet, 22; Arnoux, 21; JONES, 19; Pironi, 17; Reutemann, 15; Laffite, 12; Patrese, 7; De Angelis, 6.

Though we sent to Spain prepared to win and full of high hopes, there were warning signals flying from every flagpole: the sport was about to go back to war. The ostensible reason was that some drivers – though they hadn't been told when or where the meeting was to be held – had failed to turn up to an official briefing. M. Balestre had decided to fine all of us criminals $2000 each, and almost all of us had refused to pay – which Balestre countered by saying he would revoke our licences.

It was a heated day of practice! First, there were some teams who were going to go out and practice and some who weren't. The ones who refused to race were known as the 'loyalists' and the rest of us were branded as 'rebels'. It was a stupid quarrel which came close to wrecking the sport and took nearly a year to sort out – if it's sorted out at all! When it came to race day, there was the same controversy all over again. The Spanish organizers said the race was legal, M. Balestre said it wasn't; the loyalists – led by Ferrari, but including Renault, Alfa and Osella – refused to race, the rest of us did race.

For me, it was a lucky victory. I had three cars in front of me from the start, but all of them either broke down or crashed, and I ultimately won the race. To this day, I still can see no way in which the Spanish Grand Prix was not valid for the championship and, from a driver's point of view, I know that just as much effort, preparation – mental and physical – and risk went into that race as any other on the calendar. Not to get the 9 points I needed after winning a race was a bitter, disheartening blow, confirming my low opinion of politics in the sport, and I have neither forgiven nor forgotten. As it turned out, I did not need the Spanish points for my championship, but what if I had?

Spanish Grand Prix/Jarama/1 June/80 laps, 265.12 km.
Grid: Laffite, JONES, Pironi, Reutemann, Piquet, Prost, Zunino, Lammers, Andretti, Cheever.
Results: JONES, Mass, De Angelis, Jarier, Fittipaldi, Gaillard. (Ruled non-championship.)

As A.J. eloquently describes, the French Grand Prix arrived and, with it, a season of mutual recriminations on the political front.

Knowing that Renault had backed Balestre over Spain and that the French had combined with the Italians to put the season, and my title, into jeopardy, I went to France in a fighting mood. I not only wanted badly to win that race; I wanted my win to be a personal gesture of defiance. The Ligiers were very superior in qualifying, with Laffite and Pironi (always a dangerous rival) first and third on the grid; I was fourth.

I made a good start, raced against Arnoux and Pironi in the early stages and finally got past them, settling down into second place and starting to haul in Laffite, who was leading, inch by inch. Eventually Laffite's front tyres began to go off and I managed to pass him and win. It was probably one of my most satisfying races ever – not merely for the emotional pleasure of beating the French on their own ground, but because I think I drove one of my best ever races. Our whole team flew the Union Jack for half an hour afterwards and really tried to rub it in!

There was also a comic scene when they brought a horse up to the winner's rostrum at the end of the race. There I was with this wreath around my neck and the usual celebrations going on and I thought, That's funny, bringing a horse to the rostrum. Then they asked me if I would sit on it, and I said, 'Not on your life. I don't want to sit on a bloody horse, get it away from the rostrum.' What I didn't know then was that I'd won the horse! Well, after my lap of honour, I was having a beer or two in the motor home, winding down, when this man came back and said, 'Mr Jones, where would you like me to tie your horse up?' I thought the man was joking, so I said, 'Just tie it up to the bumper!'

Ten minutes later, I emerged from the motor home and there was this horse tied up to the back! Eventually, I had to ship it from Marseilles to Holland, then from Holland to London and thence back to Australia; it's done a few miles, that horse! But I reckon it won the lottery. If Jody had won it, it would be pasturing in a Monaco penthouse, and, if a Frog had won it, it would have wound up on a plate! Instead, it's contented on my farm in Australia and enjoying itself!

French Grand Prix/Ricard/29 June/54 laps, 313.740 km.
Grid: Laffite, Arnoux, Pironi, JONES, Reutemann, Jabouille, Prost, Piquet, Giacomelli, Depailler.
Results: JONES, Pironi, Laffite, Piquet, Arnoux, Reutemann.
Points: JONES, 28; Piquet, 25; Arnoux, Pironi, 23; Reutemann, Laffite, 16; Patrese, 7; De Angelis, 6.

Of course, we all know that what's sauce for the goose and so on. The British Grand Prix was next, and what we'd done to the French at Ricard they could do to us at Brands Hatch, and, when the two Ligiers qualified first and second on the grid, we thought it likely the French would indeed take their revenge.

Luckily for us, the Ligiers turned out to have a problem with their wheels. Pironi started well and was leading handsomely when his tyre started coming off the rim. That left Laffite in the lead, and I think he made a tactical error. He knew his tyre was going down and he could have stopped: that might have saved him a placing. Instead, he opted to soldier on and the inevitable happened: coming into Hawthorn, the tyre came completely off the rim and he went off the track. To my mind, caution is part of the driver's stock of skills.

After Laffite had dropped out, I kept the lead handsomely and won the grand prix I most wanted to win. England has become a second home for me; at home you like to prove you're a winner.

British Grand Prix/Brands Hatch/13 July/76 laps, 319.732 km.
Grid: Pironi, Laffite, JONES, Reutemann, Piquet, Giacomelli, Prost, Depailler, Andretti, Daly.
Results: JONES, Piquet, Reutemann, Daly, Jarier, Prost.
Points: JONES, 37; Piquet, 31; Arnoux, Pironi, 23; Reutemann, 20; Laffite, 16.

By now the season could be seen in some sort of perspective. A.J.'s back-to-back wins in France and England had given him a lead in the championship. And a severe problem: everyone's expectation that he was in some way a shoo-in for the title. Yet, at this point, not only was Piquet still a close challenger, consistently finishing among the front cars, but neither the Ligiers nor the Renaults could be counted out. And, so long as political issues still darkened the horizon, could anyone be sure of any-

160

thing? Watkins Glen, for instance was threatened: would A.J. need that race to win?

Germany was a bit disappointing. I got on pole right at the very end of practice, but Jabouille and his Renault swept past me on the straight going up to the chicane and I could do nothing about it for 26 laps. Then his engine blew and the lead was mine. But what the gods give, they also take away, and I suffered a puncture with only ten laps to go! But this was one of many places where the discipline and spirit of the Williams crew showed to advantage: they did a lightning tyre change in the pits, I was able to come back onto the track in third place and I kept that to the end. And the 4 points that came with it. But the disappointment remained. Victory had been in the bag. Another proof of the old adage that you never know you've won a race until you see the chequered flag!

German Grand Prix/Hockenheim/10 August/45 laps, 305.460 km.
Grid: JONES, Jabouille, Arnoux, Reutemann, Laffite, Piquet, Pironi, Rosberg, Andretti, Patrese.
Results: Laffite, Reutemann, JONES, Piquet, Giacomelli, Villeneuve.
Points: JONES, 41; Piquet, 34; Reutemann, 26; Laffite, 25; Arnoux, Pironi, 23.

People seem to think that I particularly favour the Austrian Grand Prix at Zeltweg – maybe because I won my first grand prix there – but the truth is that, though I find the circuit very beautiful, it is also one of the most dangerous, and, while the circuit is very quick, it is also subject to unpredictable weather.

As you might expect on a track surrounded by mountains, the Renaults were very quick. I made a very good start and led for a few laps, but the Renault turbos just hauled me in and passed me on the straight as though I were parked. Eventually, Arnoux's tyres went off, but Jabouille still had an excellent lead. But here I think we made a mistake. The pits didn't really keep me well-enough informed of the progress I was making against Jabouille. I was catching up – not spectacularly, but slowly – and eventually, he beat me to the finish by less than a second. If I'd been told a bit earlier, I might have launched an attack and quite possibly won. As it was, another six points helped consolidate my position, the Ligiers were now virtually out of the championship and Piquet could do no better than fifth.

Austrian Grand Prix/Zeltweg/17 August/54 laps, 320.825 km.
Grid: Arnoux, Jabouille, JONES, Reutemann, Laffite, Pironi, Piquet, Giacomelli, De Angelis, Daly.
Results: Jabouille, JONES, Reutemann, Laffite, Piquet, De Angelis.
Points: JONES, 47; Piquet, 36; Reutemann, 30; Laffite, 28; Arnoux, Pironi, 23.

The crunch of the season for A.J. came in Holland. The championship looked to be his, and it's precisely at such moments that the pressures build up. Pressures of publicity, of attention, of expectation. The man trying to catch up has little to lose; the man in front, everything.

The Dutch Grand Prix was a complete disaster for me. I was a bit twitchy because everyone was going round saying, 'Hello champ!' And I kept telling them, 'Look, don't say that, all that means is that, if I fail to finish this race and Piquet wins it, things could get very dicey indeed!' Then I had a thoroughly nasty shunt in practice when my throttle stuck coming into the Hanzerug.

I was fourth on the grid and made a tremendous start, passing the Renault on the outside going into the first right-hander. At the end of the first lap I was some two seconds clear in the lead. But then, coming back to the Hanzerug, I let the car drift a bit too wide and went off. When I came off I hit a rut, the car sank down and, by the time we'd put on new skirts, my race and my points were gone. And, as I'd feared, Piquet won the race and was now only 2 points behind me with three races to go.

Dutch Grand Prix/Zandvoort/31 August/72 laps, 306.14 km.
Grid: Arnoux, Jabouille, Reutemann, JONES, Piquet, Laffite, Villeneuve, Giacomelli, Watson, Andretti.
Results: Piquet, Arnoux, Laffite, Reutemann, Jarier, Prost.
Points: JONES, 47; Piquet, 45; Reutemann, 33; Laffite, 32; Arnoux, 29; Pironi, 23.

Imola, which came next, is definitely not − or was not then − one of my favourite circuits. The Brabham was going very well indeed, I only qualified fifth and finished second behind Nelson. The net result of which was that we were going into the last two races of the season, in America, with Piquet a point ahead of me. The only thing in my favour, apart from my conviction that the championship belonged to me, was that, with points being awarded towards the championship on the basis of the best results in the two separate halves of the season, for Piquet to win the title, he had to win the race at Montreal and I had to finish out of the first three. If he won at Montreal and I still placed high enough, then a good result at Watkins Glen, the last race, would still see me home.

Italian Grand Prix/Imola/14 September/60 laps, 300 km.
Grid: Jabouille, Arnoux, Giacomelli, Reutemann, JONES, Piquet, Villeneuve, Patrese, Andretti, Rebaque.
Results: Piquet, JONES, Reutemann, De Angelis, Rosberg, Pironi.
Points: Piquet, 54; JONES, 53; Reutemann, 37; Laffite, 32; Arnoux, 29; Pironi, 24.

I went to Montreal in a marvellous and serene mood, absolutely full of confidence. I was quickest on the first day, quickest on the second morning, and then – out of the blue, literally – Piquet found an extra second and a half! That surprised everybody, to put it mildly.

Then there came that controversial first start to the race. When the light went green, I got a better start than Nelson and took the lead, but in Montreal, after the start, you have a series of corners and, if you want to go through those corners flat, as you should, you have to take up exactly the right line. As I was in the lead and I could not see him alongside me, I took up my line. Piquet didn't back off and the result was a multiple-car, spectacular shunt. I must say, Piquet did exactly the same thing to Pironi after the re-start, but Pironi had the common sense to back off and live to fight another day.

But after the shunt – disappointingly, since I had built up a nice lead – they stopped the race and ordered a re-start. Piquet took over his spare car, I made sure I put my tyres exactly on the black marks where I had laid down rubber on the first start, and I got the jump on him again and led for two laps, but then

Piquet passed me going down the straight. But on the twenty-third lap, his engine blew.

Then I knew for sure that, as long as I conserved the car, the championship was mine. Frank put up a sign from the pits telling me Pironi had been penalized a minute for jumping the start and, realizing that I needn't race against him, I let him through and just worked on making sure the car got home. Pironi finished ahead of me but, with his penalty, dropped back to third place, and I won both the race and the championship.

The feeling is hard to describe, even now. It has to be the most fantastic feeling of all times, because when you've been working towards one goal all your life and you come around to achieving it, it is a very emotional moment indeed.

Canadian Grand Prix/Montreal/28 September/70 laps, 315 km.
Grid: Piquet, JONES, Pironi, Giacomelli, Reutemann, Rosberg, Watson, De Cesaris, Laffite, Rebaque.
Results: JONES, Reutemann, Pironi, Watson, Villeneuve, Rebaque.
Points: JONES, 62; Piquet, 54; Reutemann, 41; Laffite, 32; Arnoux, 29; Pironi, 28.

I was determined to finish off the season as I had started it, absolutely competitively: if for no other reason, to prove that champions do still try! During the first days of practice, however, I had a very down-power engine and the best I could qualify was fifth. But, come race day and the morning warm-up, we put a new engine in, and it was like night and day. I was quickest in the warm-up and thus pretty confident for the race.

In fact, I like the Glen. It's a true driver's circuit and, when the old green light came on, I did a fantastic start, jumping into second place at the first corner. But then I got into the cement they'd put down when resurfacing the track and went off into the grass. I thought, My God! I've wrecked all the skirts, I'm done for. But when I got back into the circuit and tried the car out on a couple of corners and found it was functioning all right, it became the most enjoyable, relaxed race of the year for me. I came back on ninth or tenth and, except for Giacomelli, who broke down, literally passed one car after another to win the race. Great fun! With Carlos coming in second, it was another Williams one-two and a great finish to a great season!

US Grand Prix East/Watkins Glen/5 October/59 laps, 320.665 km.
Grid: Giacomelli, Piquet, Reutemann, De Angelis, JONES, Arnoux, Pironi, Rebaque, Watson, De Cesaris.
Results: JONES, Reutemann, Pironi, De Angelis, Laffite, Andretti.
Points (Final): JONES, 67; Piquet, 54; Reutemann, 42; Laffite, 34; Pironi, 32; Arnoux, 29.

To make a perfect end to a perfect year, I went home and competed in the Australian Grand Prix, my home race, the race my father won, the race I used to go and see when I was a kid. I came home as World Champion and the crowd was absolutely marvellous, and though it was a hot race, with temperatures above 40°, I won, the car performing faultlessly and the Williams showing itself at last to my home crowd. It didn't count for the championship, which I'd already won, but, in terms of sentiment, it meant a great deal to me.

Afterword

A world championship team is a unit. A driver may win the world championship, but he can't do it without the devoted efforts of absolutely everyone: from the top, with Frank and Patrick, right down to the machine shop, the transporters, the people who take the worries off our backs and pile them on their own. I had a superb car and it was superbly looked after. Particular thanks go to Wayne Eckersley, my Australian mechanic, and his partner, John Jackson. They are solely responsible for the oustanding reliability of my car, and for my life, and without them I surely could not have won my championship. And that is true of everyone in the Williams organization: of the mechanics, too, who work on the T-car and rarely, because their car seldom gets raced, share in the glory of seeing their car win.

All season, we were one big happy family. I knew everyone was behind me 100 per cent, and this is a huge help, but especially when things are not going well. After a bad result – and we had some – to have this sort of strength and fortitude behind you is very encouraging. My heartfelt thanks to each and all.

Alan Jones's Career

Compiled by Roland Allen

Year	Car	Final Position	Score (points)
1971			
Lombard North Central Formula 3 Championship	Brabham BT28–Ford	4th	21
Forward Trust Formula 3 (Thruxton, 21 October, 15 laps)	Singleton Airo Brabham–Vegantune BT28	unplaced	
1972			
Ford Formula 3	GRD 372	unplaced	
Shell British Championship (Final at Mallory Park, 29 May)	March 723–Ford/ Vegantune	2nd	
Rothmans 50,000 (Brands Hatch, 28 August, 118 laps)	1860 cc GRD 272 Ford/BDA/Wood	20th	
1973			
John Player Formula 3 Championship	GRD 373–Ford	2nd	121
Lombard North Central Formula 3 Championship	GRD 372–Ford and GRD 373–Ford	5th	25

Year	Car	Final Position	Score (points)
1974			
John Player Formula Atlantic Championship	March 712M/732 Ford BDA/Close March 74b–Ford BDA/Richardson	4th	97
1975			
Europe Formula 5000	March V6-Ford 5000	unplaced	7 races 5 fastest laps 2 wins
1976			
SCCA/USAC Formula 5000 Championship		4th	7 races 2 wins
1978			
Can-Am (SCCA Canadian-American Challenge Cup)	Lola T-333CS	1st	2712 9 Poles 9 fastest laps 5 wins

Formula 1

Grands Prix contested (85)

Year	Car	Countries
1975	Hesketh Ford Embassy Hill Lola Ford	Spain, Monaco, Belgium, Sweden, Holland, France, Great Britain, Germany
1976	Surtees Ford	United States (West), Spain, Belgium, Monaco, Sweden, France, Great Britain, Germany, Austria, Holland, Italy, Canada, United States (East), Japan

1977	Shadow Ford	United States (West), Spain, Monaco, Belgium, Sweden, France, Great Britain, Germany, Austria, Holland, Italy, United States (East), Canada, Japan
1978	Williams Ford	Argentina, Brazil, South Africa, United States (West), Monaco, Belgium, Spain, Sweden, France, Great Britain, Germany, Austria, Holland, Italy, United States (East), Canada
1979	Williams Ford	Argentina, Brazil, South Africa, United States (West), Spain, Belgium, Monaco, France, Great Britain, Germany, Austria, Holland, Italy, Canada, United States (East)
1980	Williams Ford	Argentina, Brazil, South Africa, United States (West), Belgium, Monaco, France, Great Britain, Germany, Austria, Holland, Italy, Canada, United States (East)
1981 (to date)	Williams Ford	South Africa (non-championship), Brazil, Argentina, United States (West), San Marino, Belgium

Pole positions (6 times)

| 1979 | Great Britain, Canada, United States (East) |
| 1980 | Argentina, Belgium, Germany |

Front row (10 times)

| 1979 | Great Britain, Germany, Austria, Holland, Canada, United States (East) |
| 1980 | Argentina, Belgium, Germany, Canada |

Placed 1st (11 times)

1977	Austria
1979	Germany, Austria, Holland, Canada
1980	Argentina, France, Great Britain, Canada, United States (East)
1981	Long Beach

Placed 2nd (5 times)

1978	United States (East)
1980	Belgium, Austria, Italy
1981	Brazil

Placed 3rd (4 times)

1977	Italy
1979	United States (West)
1980	Brazil, Germany

Placed 4th (6 times)

1976	Japan
1977	Canada, Japan
1978	South Africa
1979	France
1981	San Marino

Placed 5th (5 times)

1975	Germany
1976	Belgium, Great Britain
1977	Belgium
1978	France

Placed 6th (once)

1977	Monaco

Fastest lap (8 times)

1978	United States (West), Canada
1979	Canada
1980	Argentina, France, Germany, Italy, United States (East)

Accidents/left track (8 times)

1975	Spain, Belgium
1976	Austria
1977	Germany, United States (East)
1978	Austria
1979	South Africa
1980	United States (West)

170

Laps in the lead

407

Kilometres in the lead

2158

Classifications and World Championship points

Year	Final Position	Points
1975	17th	2
1976	14th	7
1977	7th	22
1978	11th	11
1979	3rd	40
1980	1st	67